VICTORY

OVER

SIN AND TEMPTATION

"But thanks be to God,
which giveth us the victory
through our Lord Jesus Christ."

I Corinthians 15:57

Thomas Schaff

Resource *Publications*

An imprint of *Wipf and Stock Publishers*
150 West Broadway • Eugene OR 97401

Resource *Publications*
an imprint of Wipf and Stock Publishers
150 West Broadway
Eugene, Oregon 97401

Victory Over SIn and Temptation
By Schaff, Thomas

ISBN: 1-57910-983-7
Publication date: June, 2002

Victory over Sin and Temptation

Preface

Dear Reader,

We, as all people, are sinners by nature and practice. Would not that fact make our attempt to write a book about sin and temptation presumptuous? Would not that fact discredit the value of any insight we try to offer into the nature of sin and temptation? Would not that fact disqualify us from giving any helpful counsel to others who seek to gain victory over them? If what we write is based primarily upon our experience and personal reflection, then our words cannot be trusted and must not be a guide. However, we are all commanded to seek the perfect wisdom of the sinless One, who explains all we need to know in His Word, the Bible. And it is our desire to faithfully and clearly bring the Bible's message concerning sin and temptation, in order that you may live a life that honors the Lord Jesus Christ and know the joy of obedience to His will.

We do not write about sin and temptation because we think we are so holy and so in control of ourselves that sin is no longer a problem in our lives, as if sin and temptation are issues of the past we have completely resolved. We do not expect people to read and heed these words because we claim to have finally attained victory over all our sins and therefore offer perfect wisdom and counsel. Instead, we write these things as experts in sin. Sadly, we have lots of experience with sin and continue to gain more experience as we struggle daily with sin and temptation (Psalm 38:4-6, 40:12). And yet, as time goes by, by grace we understand more and more of the Bible's message about what is true and false about sin and temptation. Day after day we learn to value all that the Bible says about them; and it has a great deal to say about sin and temptation. Equipped with biblical insight, we can experience victories over sin and temptation, victories that God gives to us according to His gracious will (Rom. 7:24,25, I Cor. 15:57).

We are motivated to write what the Bible teaches about sin and temptation because we recognize the common, immediate and abiding struggle we all have with them. We write these things because we see the present and eternal peril that is a consequence of sin. There is no more important question we could answer in life than, "Does what I think and do about sin, especially about my own personal sin, reveal if I am saved?"

For all these reasons and more, we present these words because we believe that a clear and accurate understanding of sin and temptation is an important foundation for assurance of salvation and for leading a life that both honors God and brings spiritual benefit to others. To that end, we pray that these words may result in your increased faithfulness. And we pray that these words may give you courage that is a consequence of knowing for sure what you believe. The spiritual strength that comes from such conviction is especially needed in the face of the numerous, compelling and bewildering attractions of sin that are a part of this modern world.

May you, by God's grace, be free from the condemnation and penalty of sin. May you, by His wisdom and strength, gain victory over the power of sin and temptation. May you, according to His promise, live before the Lord in His heavenly Kingdom separated from the presence of sin forever.

Sincerely,

Thomas Schaff

Introduction

A positive word

Notice the title of this book is not "Sin and Temptation," but "Victory over Sin and Temptation." It is true that a large portion of this book focuses upon the embarrassing and offensive subject of sin. However, despite its emphasis upon such a sad and dark theme, it contains a positive message. Its purpose is to help us properly understand what the Bible teaches about sin so that we can discover God's plan for victory over it. The Bible explains how we can submit to that plan and how God gives us the victory thereby.

We cannot avoid sin. Sin surrounds us and dwells within us. And yet, we can take courage. There is reason to hope. The good news is that there is a way to overcome sin's power and influence. The Bible's message about sin and temptation is meant for our personal profit and the God's honor.

Two extreme views

I was motivated to write this book because, after hundreds of conversations with people, both in person and through correspondence, I recognized how confused they were about sin and temptation. I was concerned because their confusion often led to fear or belligerence, attitudes that reveled they did not truly grasp the Bible's message of sin. They appreciated neither the horror of sin nor the Gospel's promise of rescue and relief. I also noticed that many times people's confusion about sin and temptation led them to strange, unbiblical doctrines as well as behavior that harmed both themselves and others. Their confusion usually was expressed in two extreme views of how Christians relate to God's law.

The first extreme view I want to examine is based upon the idea that, because salvation is by grace apart from the law (Rom. 3:28), because it is independent of the work of man (Eph. 2:8,9), Christians do not have to concern themselves too much about obeying the Bible's commands. This view is sometimes supported by a liberal interpretation of Galatians 5:1 that says, "Stand fast in the liberty wherewith Christ hath made us free, and be not entangled again with a yoke of bondage." The idea is labeled as "Christian liberty" and can be expressed as "free from the law, oh happy condition," in the sense that "freedom" means Christians are free to indulge themselves in the amusements and social habits of the people of the world.

The fruit of this point of view is a spiritually or morally casual life, indistinguishable in many respects from the life of an unsaved person. This extreme view promotes the attitude that living by grace means obedience to God's law is not very important. This view has sometimes been labeled "easy-believism." That is, it is a belief that is easy to adopt because it is accompanied by no obligation to conform to the restrictions or expectations found in the Bible. However, such a view is very wrong. It an extreme view that is fundamentally a denial of God's grace and power as well as an excuse for self-indulgence.

People who hold to this extreme view sometimes say, "It really doesn't matter how holy I live. Afer all, sincerity counts. Even though I keep breaking my resolution to turn from this bad habit, I am trying. That is all that matters." That expresses an incomplete understanding of a Christian life.

The danger of such a view is illustrated by Lot. Though he was a true believer, he chose to live in wicked, spiritually corrosive Sodom and witnessed the sad consequences of a family that lived far from God's will (Gen. 19:26, 36).

The second extreme view I want to consider is based upon the idea that, because the work of grace will show in Christians' character and behavior (James 3:18), Christians' strict obedience to the Bible's commands is both required and expected, with very little exception. This view is sometimes supported by a verse such as I Peter 1:15, " but as he which hath called you is holy, so be ye holy in all manner of conversation." The idea can be expressed as, "if it walks like a duck and talks like a duck, then it is a duck," in the sense that a person's outward behavior is an unfailing, accurate measure of his soul, and any variance from God's commands calls into question his salvation.

One fruit of this point of view is pride in the hearts of people who think they have achieved compliance to God's law and a critical attitude toward other people whom they estimate have not. Another fruit of this point of view is alarm in the hearts of people who recognize that they do not measure up to God's holiness. This view has sometimes been labeled "perfectionism" or "moralism." In this view, salvation is accompanied by a life that conforms to the restrictions or expectations found in the Bible with few or minor exceptions. This view includes the attitude that as soon as an area of non-compliance is detected in a person's life, his salvation is suspect. However, such a view also is wrong. It is an extreme view that is fundamentally a gospel of works, inasmuch as it teaches people's relationship to God is determined or maintained by a their performance.

As we shall learn in this book, the Bible's view is different from both of those extreme views. The quick answer to all of this confusion is, "Yes, outward obedience must and will be seen in the lives of people who are saved. However, outward obedience is neither complete or as consistent as it should be, or as it will be in Heaven." In the final analysis, it is not a person's record of obedience, but rather it is a person's inner "want to," or heart desire that is the true testimony to his salvation. That desire only is seen by and known to God and the person himself.

It is not too much to say that a person's motive is more important than the acts he performs. His godly motive will be reflected more and more in his performance, as over time he grows in his understanding of the Bible and in his ability to do that which he understands is right. There must be some present obedience in a Christian's life and there must be growth in obedience. But his record of performance will always be marred with many faults due to the ever present desires of his flesh and due to the baggage he carries with him from his rebellious past. And as we will learn, it is not God's will that, on earth, Christian's perfectly express the holy desire to obey He has created in their hearts. God reserves that perfect, outward compliance for their life in Heaven.

Therefore, we must avoid the judgmental attitude that characterizes the second extreme view of the law and Christian life. We cannot accurately evaluate the spiritual condition of some one else based upon our observations alone, nor should we try. While we are led to pray for other people based upon what we see in their lives, the Bible expects us leave the state of their souls in God's hands and take heed to our own lives (Matt. 7:1-3, I Tim. 4:16).

How to Use this Book

How this book helps you depends, in part, upon your situation at the moment and your goals. If you want immediate counsel to help you gain victory over a sin that is presently troubling you, then you may profit from reading chapters 3 and 4. If you are interested in a more complete explanation of the nature and character of sin, in order to understand how serious a problem it is, then turn to the rest of this book.

We must caution you before you read this book. There are dangers associated with reading something about sin, even if what you read is true and faithful to the Bible. For one thing, increasing your knowledge about sin, ironically, may promote the sin of pride (I Cor. 8:1-2). Secondly, if you have gained a measure of success overcoming some sins in your life, you may become frustrated and impatient with people who are still struggling with similar sins. You even may condemn them (Matt. 7:3, Rom. 14:3-6). Thirdly, you may pay a great deal of attention to accurately understanding what the Bible teaches about sin, or any other doctrine for that matter, and forget to do what the Bible commands (Matt. 23:3). In other words, learning a lot of true things about the nature of sin and how to successfully deal with it does not in itself mean you have achieved victory over it.

Perhaps the best advice we could give to you before you read this book is to point out that your attempts to deal with sin must be a natural extension of your daily devotion to God. Victory over sin is a result of your personal, faithful walk with God. You must keep in mind that the solution to anyone's sin problem begins and ends with God Himself. He provides the insight, motivation, strategy, tactics, power, and eventual success. Therefore, reading this book will help you in your struggle against sin only to the extent that you trust and love God, call upon Him consistently in prayer and spend time studying and meditating upon His Word.

Chapter 1 Is sin real?

The purpose of this chapter is to force us to face the reality of sin. There are so many more pleasant things we would rather think about. It is tempting to ignore sin and hope that it would go away, like a bad dream from which we wake up. But sin will not disappear. Sin is firmly bound to our lives and has become a part of who we are. Worse than that, we must open our eyes to the fact that sin is a very real enemy that deceitfully seeks to keep us from all that is pure and good. In fact, it seeks to destroy us. And yet sin is not a foe so formidable and unconquerable that we can do nothing more than hide from it. We can gain victory over sin. But the first step toward victory is facing the fact that sin is real.

1. An irrelevant idea?

Most people admit, if only to themselves, that they are not perfect and that they sometimes can think, say and do things that are surprisingly harmful to others as well as to themselves. Yet most people either ignore the suggestion that their behavior is sin or despise the idea of sin as a vulgar subject that is not an appropriate topic of conversation in polite, civilized society. They are unwilling to agree with the Bible that their problems are the result of sin, especially their own personal sin. In fact, according to Proverbs 14:9, "Fools make a mock at sin." That is, people for whom the Bible is not the highest or final authority consider the idea of sin to be a joke. They think of the concept of sin as something laughable, not out of humor but out of scorn and derision. They do not take sin seriously because for them it is unreal. Their objective is to justify their claim that the idea of sin is irrelevant to their own lives.

For example, some people think that the idea of sin is part of the myths which the ancients invented, as they attempted to explain the offensive behavior of men. Other people think that sin is a leftover notion from a prudish Victorian past. For all these people, the idea of sin is an historical museum piece. They dismiss it as an old-fashion concept with no connection to modern reality. In another example, some people think sin is a belief that comes out of a narrow-minded interpretation of one "religious" book, the Bible. Or people think that sin is a word used by bizarre or perverted religious fanatics who seek to control the lives of others. Therefore, these people have decided that sin not only is unreal, it also is a harmful idea that ought to be condemned and abandoned. As always, they view sin as an idea that does not apply to them.

2. As real as death

Interestingly, the Bible does not attempt to prove the reality of sin with rigorous logic or persuasive reasoning. Instead, the Bible links sin, a fuzzy or vague idea for many people, to a concrete and specific fact of their existence, a fact which they cannot explain away. The Bible ties sin to the undeniable fact of death. The Bible says in Romans 5:12, "Wherefore, as by one man sin entered into the world, and **death by sin**; and so death passed upon all men, for that all have sinned." From the words "and death by (actually, 'through') sin," we learn that death "entered into the world" through the door called sin. In other words, the presence of death in this universe is dependent upon the reality of sin. The point is that people know sin exists because they can observe and in fact will experience death.

According to the Bible, since death exists, sin does, too. That is, sin is as real as death. Whether we wish to think of death in physical terms, spiritual terms, or both, its presence in the universe is the evidence of the existence of sin. Therefore, instead of an imaginary product of human invention that has no connection to people's present lives, sin is as real as the most relevant event of all, death.

Most people object to the connection which Romans 5:12 makes between death and sin. People like to think of death as a neutral event. For them, death is nothing more than the end of physical life. However, the Bible explains that death has a spiritual dimension. Death is not just biological disintegration. It also is the evidence of sin. As we learned, death exists as a consequence of the fact that sin exists. In addition to that, the words "by (or 'through') one man" in Romans 5:12 insist that the sin which results in death is the fault of humankind. Although God claims the credit for bringing the curse of death into the universe, inasmuch as death is His just answer to sin (Gen. 2:17), humankind receives the blame for the entrance of sin, that in turn let in death.

3. As real as history

The reality of sin is based not only upon its link to the undisputed reality of death, but also upon the fact that it has an origin and a documented history in real time and space. God created a universe that was very good. It was imaginatively designed, well engineered and cleverly constructed; and it operated in perfect harmony with His will. It was without sin. Then, at a real moment in time, in a real place on earth, a real particular human being disobeyed God. That was the origin of human sin. After the first man, Adam, sinned, he experienced immediate death in his soul. His flesh was thoroughly infected by sin, which subsequently controlled his desires and behavior. In time, his flesh died too. In addition, God altered the world in which men lived. The world became a hostile environment. Through God's curse, the world shared in man's experience of deterioration and death. To tell the story of the real world and its inhabitants is to tell the story of the real sin which has played a major role in the violent conflicts that mark the course of human events throughout time.

4. A vain denial of reality

Unsaved people are unwilling to admit the reality of sin. They reject the reality of sin because they are reluctant to deny themselves the gratification of their sinful appetites. They also reject the reality of sin because they do not want to face their accountability before God. Sadly, when they reject the reality of sin, they also reject the only truth that could free them from its grip and its consequences (John 8:32-36). And yet, daily they must face the deterioration and decay which accompanies sin. For that reason, they still seek both an explanation for their world's brokenness and a promise of deliverance from its sorrows. However, rather than go to God for His true perspective of reality and His solution to solve their real problems, people look to each other for wisdom and help. What do they find? In Psalm 108:12 we read, "Give us help from trouble: for vain is the help of man." As this verse points out, what people offer to help themselves understand and cope with all that is wrong in this world is vain.

Man's help is vain, both in the sense that the words he uses to explain sin are egotistical and in the sense that his counsel to deal with sin is worthless. First of all, let us think about the fact that man's help is vain in the sense that his words are egotistical. II Peter 2:18 makes the observation that the words of help unsaved authors and teachers offer to whomever will listen are nothing more than "great swelling words of vanity." The words of unsaved authors and teachers are "words of vanity" in the sense that they are self-flattering and self-justifying "swelling words" designed to inflate their own pride as well as the pride of their listeners. Unsaved authors and teachers never abandon the conceit that people have a spark of goodness within themselves. They continue the fantasy that people must believe in themselves and have faith in mankind.

In addition to that, man's words are egotistical in that they are self-serving. II Peter states that when men offer words of help, they use words that "allure through the lusts of the flesh" (II Peter 2:18). That is, their words promote and support the sinful passions of both the authors and their readers. Unsaved authors are popular and well spoken of because they express the sinful philosophy and yearnings of "wantonness" that fills and controls the hearts of all unsaved people who read their literature.

Secondly, man's help is vain in the sense that his counsel is worthless. II Peter 2:18 points out that unsaved authors and teachers "promise liberty" from the corruption that is everyone's common experience. Yet they remain as bound to their sin and its corrupting effects as the people who hear them. That is, the words of help unsaved authors and teachers offer are vain in the sense that the words are futile. The words have no power. They are weak words of deceit (Rom. 16:18, I Cor. 3:19-20).

For centuries gifted authors have been admired and honored for their mastery of language and for the accuracy of their insight into the misery and heartache all human's share. These authors have become famous because they have skillfully written beautiful and poignant descriptions of the sadness and despair people endure, suffering the wounds inflicted by themselves and others. And yet, their work is futile because their stories end there. Authors of great literature offer no real hope for a change in the human condition (Psalm 108:12, Jer. 17:5,6, Col. 2:23, II Peter 2:19). These authors may have correctly exposed men's foolish behavior in dramas, essays, poetry and novels. They may have described the sinful behavior of men with skill and art. They may have mocked the sinful behavior of men with perceptive irony and humor. They may have condemned the sinful behavior of men with bitterness and anger. However, their accurate descriptions of the folly of men are superficial. Few, if any, are able or willing to see the root of the matter. They do not recognize the sinful, wicked nature of people and refuse to recognize the grip sin has upon their hearts. Also, they do not acknowledge the curse of God in response to sin that all people must bear. That is, few, if any, recognize the quarrel all men have with God.

The shelves of bookstores and libraries sag under the weight of many books. Some may contain eloquent laments about the human condition. However, in none can we find the wisdom or the power needed for relief from the present enslavement to personal sin. Some may offer self-improvement plans. However, in none can we find the wisdom or the power needed for relief from the conflict and oppression that are part of a wicked society. Some may promote expensive social projects or advocate improved political or judicial systems. However, in none can we find the wisdom or the power needed for relief from the threat of judgment for sin. The reason is that the authors choose to ignore or deny both sin and the threat of condemnation. The authors of great literature leave themselves and their readers as they are, hopelessly immersed in their sin and its consequences.

Sometimes authors do recognize the fallibility of all men, including themselves. However, they try to cleverly explain away the problem. For example, rather than admit the existence of individual personal sin, they present human failing as a common problem, shared by society as a whole. The guilt they describe is so diffused that no one really feels personally liable or accountable for any particular act of wickedness. As an another example, they criticize and mock the sins of a few especially prominent or notorious people in society. In that way, authors and their readers feel self-righteous, inasmuch as they have not taken part in the specific transgressions they condemn. Not only that, by focussing upon the prejudice and cruelty of some people against others, authors honor the victims as innocent, oppressed people. Authors desire to ennoble a part of the human race thereby, and retain a measure of human glory and dignity. Yet in the drama of sin no one is innocent. There are no victims. All people are villains. Some may be more successful at sinning because they are more clever or have more opportunity and so are able to assert their wicked ways over other people more effectively. But all people are willful sinners, the oppressed as well as the oppressors, committing acts of violence against God and His law (Matt. 11:12, Luke 16:16-18, Rom. 3:10-12).

5. The value of seeing what is real

Unsaved people hate the Bible's message that sin is real because sin is an embarrassment to them. They think better of themselves. People also hate the Bible's message that sin is a deadly foe too strong for them to conquer. It is a wound to their pride that they cannot solve their problems on their own. Furthermore, people hate the Bible's message that they are accountable to God for their own personal sins. They do not want God's control over them or the punishment that He demands for their disobedience. So people prefer to think of sin as fiction, something remote and unconnected to their lives.

However, sin is not an obscure philosophical construction or an irrelevant religious doctrine. Sin is as real as the world it contaminates and corrupts. In fact, recognizing the reality of sin is the beginning point from which we make sense out of this oftentimes bewildering and painful world.

Even though most people do not acknowledge the reality of sin, they still see or experience destruction and death. Most people, then, turn away from or dismiss God in anger and fear. They decide God is an incompetent or evil Creator, or claim that He is unreal. When most people cry out, it is usually to blame God and justify themselves. They conveniently suppress the evidence that the cause of most of their troubles is found within themselves.

Sadly, because most people dismiss the reality of sin, they will never really enjoy all the blessings of love, harmony, peace and hope for which they yearn. There is no picture more pathetic than that of people who are wounded and diseased, confused and frightened, bitter and sad, yet defiantly shaking their fist at the One who comes to them with an honest message of sin and the comforting promise of the Gospel, which alone can give them hope. But unless people are willing to face the truth of the reality of personal sin, they are unwilling to face the only thing that can help them.

In contrast to that, people who recognize the reality of sin find answers to the most disturbing and frightening questions of life. They alone find the means and power to gain victory over sin's dominion. Only with a God-given understanding of the reality of sin, can people be filled with true joy as well as unshakable peace and contentment.

Chapter 2: What is sin?

The purpose of this chapter is to present a correct and clear explanation of sin. Sin is such a familiar word. It is part of the vocabulary of most people and used in their conversations. Yet people seldom have a clear idea of what sin is, nor do they understand sin to be a serious threat to their lives. Therefore, we should be grateful to God for His Word, the Bible, which alone provides us with an accurate understanding of sin. God's Word also eliminates the many confusing and wrong notions about sin that interfere with our attempts to gain victory over it.

1. Sin is a problem to solve

As cheerless and uncomfortable as the subject of sin may be, what the Bible teaches us about it is a source of real hope, comfort and joy. Life is not just the sum of all the cruelty and pain we see around us. This sometimes frustrating, disgusting and frightening existence is not a mindless, pointless joke. The good news of the Bible is that all the sadness exists for a reason. The reason is that sin entered into a perfect universe through the disobedience of the first man, Adam (Rom. 5:12). Adam was without sin when he was created. But Adam subsequently became a sinner, a human with a sin-corrupted nature. Since kind begets kind (Gen. 1:24-25), all of Adam's descendants are sinners, too, revealing their corrupt nature by the sins they commit every day. Thus, the Bible teaches that sin and its effects are not part of the original design of the universe. A universe with sin is not the way it was supposed to be. Sin is not an annoyance to tolerate or a menace to accept. Our hope is not limited to minimizing sin's influence and effects. Rather, sin is a problem to be solved, and its contamination is a stain to be cleansed.

From one point of view, we can say that success in dealing with sin is based upon the fact that sin is not man's problem to solve. It is God's problem. Sin is not God's problem in the sense that sin is God's fault or that God must control sin in His own life. God never thinks, says or does anything that is contrary to His own law. Rather, sin is God's problem in the sense that after sin entered into God's perfect creation, it was up to Him to help Adam and his descendants out of the mess in which they found themselves. God did not have to do that. However, God took man's problem seriously, and decided to make man's sin His problem to solve. Since no man could or would solve his own or anyone else's sin problem (Isaiah 59:16, 63:5, Rev. 5:4,5), God had to step in or nothing would have been done. Therefore, God obligated Himself to help sinners. The Bible states that before the foundation of the world, before any man was around to participate, God designed, prepared and provided for His Gospel plan to solve man's sin problem (II Tim. 1:9). Wonderfully, sin, our own personal sin, is a problem that God Himself faces, resolves and removes in Jesus Christ.

We can compare the importance of attempting to answer the question "What is sin?" to the value of a medical diagnosis. In order to have any hope of finding a remedy for a disease, we must be sure that we accurately identify the disease and understand both its nature and behavior. We can dispute or ignore any pathological evaluation of our condition we do not like. We can refuse the prescribed therapy, calling the evaluation and treatment unnecessary. But if we do, any sickness we have will remain. How much more serious is our sin problem! Sin is the deadliest disease of all, for it results in eternal death in Hell under the wrath of God. The spiritual pain and consequence of sin are far more horrible than any physical malady anyone has ever suffered. If we suppress the Bible's penetrating diagnosis of our sin problem, we do so to our eternal peril. The Bible calls us to be sure we know the truth about our sin as well as the truth about the help that God alone has provided in the Savior, Jesus Christ, the only One who can remove the penalty and power of sin (Rom. 8:3-4).

Without a proper understanding of sin, people are led to a life of fear and license. Without a proper understanding of sin, the Christian life becomes a hollow fad that is just so much religious music, trite clichés and Jesus symbols.

On the other hand, with a correct understanding of sin and a proper appreciation of the problem that it is, life has meaning and purpose. The Bible's idea of sin gets to the heart of why Jesus came to earth and of what destiny each person can expect to face. That is, what people think about sin will determine what they do about their sin problem and how successful their efforts will be.

2. Sin is disobedience

So far, we have discussed many things about sin. However, we have not yet presented a clear and precise definition of sin, which is a necessary prerequisite for understanding it. To that end, let us begin our understanding of sin with the observation that the Bible states sin is a label for what we **do**. In I John 3:4, we read, "Whosoever committeth sin transgresseth also the law: for sin is the transgression of the law." In simplest words, sin is **disobedience** of God's law. We begin our understanding of sin with an objective description of performance. If what we do or do not do contradicts God's law, we have sinned. A strict application of I John 3:4 leads us to state that the word "sin" is a label that identifies a person's deeds which differ from the expressed statements in God's law.

Obviously, any list of sins includes overt actions which can be measured against God's law. But the thoughts of a person's heart also can be sin (Prov. 24:9), as well as his speech which expresses his heart (Matt. 12:34). Thoughts can be sin in the sense that they are attitudes forbidden by God's law. For example, they can include an attitude toward God such as unbelief. Or they can include an attitude toward self such as pride. Or they can include attitudes toward others such as anger or lust. Thoughts also can be sin in the sense that they are a wrong view of the Bible and what it teaches. That is, if what a person thinks about the message of the Bible is not in strict accord to what is true, those thoughts are sin. That means any doctrine which is not accurate or correct is sin.

Notice that there really is no distinction between transgressions of deed or doctrine. It is all sin. This is true because everything is compared to God's one standard. This is also true because what a person thinks cannot be separated from what he does. On one hand, what a person thinks shapes his words and actions. What a person thinks about the Bible's message of creation, the atonement, and the final judgment directly effects what he says and does. On the other hand, the words a person loves to say and actions that a person loves to do will influence him to modify his doctrine in order to justify his behavior. A crooked life spawns and nourishes crooked thoughts about what the Bible teaches.

We must mention that sin is independent of a person's intentions. Sin is a word that identifies any behavior of a person that is different from the commands stated in God's law, regardless of his ignorance or misunderstanding of that law, independent of his purpose (Lev. 5:17). Any thought, word or deed that does not perfectly match the commandments of God is sin. We also must point out that sin is independent of a person's emotions. Sin is not a matter of feeling but of fact. When a person disobeys God, he may or may not have "guilty feelings," but he is guilty just the same. His guilt is established by measuring his behavior against God's law.

This concrete and specific understanding of sin is unacceptable to unsaved people. It is a hateful reminder of their clear obligation to obey God, as well as a frightening reminder of their accountability to God for their disobedience.

At this point, we must be careful. A performance-based understanding of sin must not lead us to think wrong ideas about sin. I John 3:4 does not imply that, if we can control our behavior such that we outwardly conform to God's law or avoid any outward disobedience of it, we are free of sin. We cannot decide, based upon an examination of our outward performance alone, whether anything we do is a sin or not. In other words, behavior that is in agreement with God's law includes, but is not limited to, an outward compliance with it. The reason is that, as we have alluded to and as we shall explain, our outward behavior cannot be separated from who we are as a person inside.

3. Sin is deliberate disobedience

To our understanding of sin as a label for performance we should add the observation that the Bible also teaches sin is a label for what we **want** to do. According to James 4:17, "Therefore to him that knoweth to do good, and doeth it not, to him it is sin." Sin is a label that describes a person's disobedient behavior in light of what he knows he ought to do. A person sins fully aware of what he does because that is what he wants to do. Therefore, James 4:17 adds the idea that sin is a **deliberate** refusal to obey God. That is, sin labels a person's willful behavior, his intentional disobedience of God's law (Rom. 1:21).

From this point of view, we understand sin to be a deliberate assertion of a person's will in opposition to God's will. God says, "Do this. Don't do that." People who sin respond outwardly or in their heart, "Phooey. I'll do what I want instead." Sin is what men do or do not do based upon a wicked and self-centered heart that says "Leave me alone and let me live my own life as I want. I am my own boss. I want to fulfill my own plans." Sin labels what a person does, motivated by his rebellious desire to replace God's will with his own objectives and plans. Sin can be compared to the actions of a little child who throws a temper-tantrum. Blind to the folly and results of his actions, a stubborn, willful child demands his own way, even if his actions will clearly result in damage and harm to himself and others. Similarly, we can say that sin is a person's juvenile, out-of-control pursuit of his own selfish desires.

Since a proper understanding of sin includes the recognition that a person knows what is right yet refuses to comply, perhaps we should ask, "Who knows what is right?" Many people know what is right from a limited exposure to God's word. But everybody knows what is right from the law that is written on their hearts, from their consciences (Rom. 2:14-15). The point is that Adam was not ignorant of his responsibility, and no man since has been ignorant of God's demands or of his own accountability before God for his disobedience. The sinful disobedience which all men demonstrate exhibits their deliberate, stubborn and rebellious desire to disobey God. They simply do not want to do what God says.

Some people object to this understanding of men's intentions. According to their view, men want to obey and try to obey but are not quite able to measure up to the perfect demands of God's law. They appeal to a verse such as Romans 3:28, which states, "For all have sinned, and come short of the glory of God." Their idea is that men try in their sinful way to do what God says, but come up short. We can illustrate their idea with the picture of a man who has shot an arrow at a target and missed the mark.

But this is a wrong way to think of both Romans 3:23 and sin. People do indeed lack the glory of God, as this verse states. But if we use the same illustration, then a more correct picture would be of a man who deliberately turns around and faces the opposite way from the target. In fact, the man in his perverseness breaks the bow and arrow, having no desire to hit the target. That is the message of Romans 3:10-18. Romans 3:23 is not a comment on people's ineffective efforts to achieve the standard of God's glorious righteousness. Sin is a deliberate act of disobedience. Outside of Christ, people **do not even want to** obey God. It takes the grace of God to turn anyone around so that he faces God's righteous law. It takes the grace of God to cause anyone to seek the glory of God through humble submission to the Gospel.

How devious people are in their attempts to achieve their own desires in opposition to the will of God! For example, people often base their ethics upon the situation at the moment. They so easily negotiate and compromise any standards that guide their behavior because they refuse to recognize the absolute requirements of God's law. This is illustrated by a man who lies on his tax reports to his government, with whose policies and practices he does not agree. This also is illustrated by a woman who destroys her unborn baby through an abortion in order to protect her own life. People are motivated by a desire to be free to do what they want, as well as by an ambition to turn any situation to their own advantage.

In another example, people often measure their own behavior by comparing it with the behavior of somebody else and conclude that when they sometimes do sin it is not really so bad. This is illustrated by people who are horrified at the murders reported on the front page of their newspaper and so feel their own anger and resentments are far less serious, even inconsequential. But that comparison is a pointless exercise. As we have learned, when people sin they act in a deliberate, willful and hateful rebellion against God's law. God's law is the perfect and uncompromising standard to which men must compare their thoughts, words and deeds. And as we learned, when people sin they demonstrate that they simply do not want to do what God requires of them. Sin is a conflict of wills, theirs against God's.

4. Sin and the law

In support of the idea that sin is deliberate disobedience to God's will, we can briefly look at the phrases "break the commandments" and "break the law," which are found in the Bible (Matt. 5:19, Rom. 2:23) and used in common conversation today. No one really can break a law, especially God's law, in the way he might break a porcelain vase or a wooden stick. The phrase, "break the law," does not mean that we are able to damage the law. We cannot reduce its strength or authority over us. Instead, we can understand these words in the following way. After God created Adam, He made a contract with him. One part of the contract can be summarized as, "Obey me and live." Eventually, Adam disobeyed God. We could say that Adam "broke the terms" of the contract that he was expected to fulfill in order to maintain a right relationship with God and continue to experience His blessings. Today unsaved people are under the same obligation to obey that Adam was. However, unlike Adam originally was, they are spiritually dead. And yet, it is a fact that they still have an obligation to do what God commands. It also is a fact that they disobey. Therefore, they are liable as people who have "broken the law."

Incidentally, we should mention that even though some people may be consciously unaware of the written law of God, they are not free from the obligation to obey it. The contract that God made with Adam, that God many years later expressed in propositional statements in His Word, applies to all men. Men's accountability before God is independent of the quantity of God's law that is revealed to them.

Therefore, it is not correct to say that a certain remote tribe of people who never heard the Word of God are held to a different standard than those who have read the Bible. Members of that tribe are held to the same standard as are all men (Rom. 2:11-16).

In addition to that, it might seem that since sin is disobedience of God's law, sin exists because the law exists, and if the law did not exist then neither would sin (Rom. 4:15). Or as I Corinthians 15:56 puts it, "the strength of sin is the law." It is true that sin exists because the law exists (Rom. 7:7,8). But that does not imply that the law is the cause of men's sin. Nor does it imply that the solution to sin is to get rid of the law. Both of those ideas are the common thinking of unsaved people. But they are wrong.

We must disconnect the law and sin from any cause-and-effect relationship. The law is an independent statement of God's perfect standard of behavior (Psalm 19:7), to which the behavior of all people is compared. It is like a perfectly straight metal rod which reveals the crookedness of any stick to which it is compared. Whether a stick is crooked or straight is a fact of its shape, independent of any other object. A stick does not become crooked when it is held next to a straight rod. Similarly, people are the kind of creatures who behave in a certain way and the law simply reveals what they do, just as a light beam cast into a dark room reveals what already exists there (John 3:19,20, Rom. 5:20, Gal. 3:19, Eph. 5:13). The idea is that the law exposes sin. It does not cause sin.

Besides, removing the law makes no sense. The law would cease to exist only if God would cease to exist. The law has no existence or meaning independent of God Himself. The reason is far deeper than the fact that God is the author of the law. The standard of behavior that is described in the law is not a set of self-existent, autonomous rules with an authority above God, to which He also must conform. The law is really a description of God Himself, how He thinks, what He says, and what He does. God is who He is. He has a character that causes Him to think, say and do things in a certain way, and the law reveals what that is. In fact, the law is a synonym for God, inasmuch as He calls Himself "the Word" (John 1:1, Rev. 19:13) and He calls His Word "the law" (Isaiah 1:10, Mal. 4:4 with Deut. 5:5). The issue is that God expects from people, whom He has created in His own image, the same standard of behavior that He expects from Himself. That is what He means in a verse such as I Peter 1:6, "be ye holy even as I am holy." So it makes no sense to suggest that we get rid of the law, because desiring to get rid of the law is the same as wanting to get rid of God, which is an impossible and illogical demand.

Chapter 3: How can I gain victory over sin?

The purpose of this chapter is to present the right principles, attitudes and methods for successfully dealing with sin. Victory over sin is what God wants for His people. Victory over sin is what God expects in His peoples' lives. Therefore, victory over sin is what they also should desire and expect.

Understanding Colossians 3: God's program for dealing with sin

As we search for help to gain victory over sin, we could glean wisdom from any part of the Bible. But the counsel God gives in Colossians 3 is complete and easy to grasp. Therefore, we shall use this chapter to direct and guide our investigation.

Verses 1 and 2 state two principles that form the foundation of God's plan for dealing with sin. In order to be as clear as possible, we will state the first principle and then begin our analysis of verse 1. Similarly, we will state the second principle before studying verse 2. After we have looked at these two verses, we will briefly leave Colossians 3 and develop a few important companion ideas. After that, we will return to our analysis of the chapter, which explains and illustrates the two principles. Our examination of the rest of the verses will less extensive than that of verses 1 and 2, but we will spend enough time to highlight a few important points.

Colossians 3:1, "If ye then be risen with Christ, seek those things which are above, where Christ sitteth on the right hand of God."

The first of two fundamental principles that form the foundation of God's plan for gaining victory over sin is:

A true born again believer **can** turn from sin and obey God.

Now let us look at the details of verse 1 that lead up to and support this principle.

The word "if" begins a conditional statement. That means the counsel of the chapter does not apply to everybody. It is reserved for someone who meets the requirements that are given in the verse. The instruction of Colossians 3 is only for someone who is "risen with Christ."

The word "ye" is plural. It is an inclusive word, gathering together all people who are "risen with Christ." The instruction of the chapter is for everyone who is "risen with Christ," without exception. There are no people who are "risen with Christ" to whom this counsel does not apply. In other words, if someone is "risen with Christ," they will follow this counsel and eventually will successfully deal with their sins.

The word "then" implies a connection between the contents of Colossians 3 and the contents of Colossians 1 and 2. That is, chapter 3 reminds us of and continues some previous ideas. One idea is expressed by the words, "Who hath delivered us from the power of darkness and hath translated us into the kingdom of his dear Son" (Col. 1:13), implying that those people who are "risen with Christ" are under a new authority, Christ's and no longer Satan's. Another idea is expressed as, "and you, being dead in your sins and the uncircumcision of your flesh, hath he quickened together with him, having forgiven you all trespasses" (Col. 2:13). This implies that those people who are "risen with Christ," in addition to a judicial pardon, have received a life they never had before. It is not a life separate and independent from God. It is Christ's eternal life in them (Col. 1:27, Gal. 2:20). Thus, those who are "risen with Christ" are expected to be different than they were before, both inside and outside (II Cor. 5:17).

The word "then" also introduces a conclusion. If, as Colossians 1 and 2 explained, Jesus has the wisdom, authority and power to remove His people from the dominion of Satan (Col. 1:13, 2:15), if Jesus separated His people from the penalty (Col. 1:14) and power of sin (Col. 2:11,12), if Jesus is sufficient for all His people's needs (Col. 2:10), if, in contrast, human attempts to deal with sin, based upon philosophy, empty promises, vain traditions, and a physical focus do not help people deal with sin in an honorable way (Col. 2:23), either now or at the end of time, "then" they should seek His help as they face the challenges of their own personal sins. That is, chapter 3 explains the value of Jesus' solution for His people's daily struggle with sin.

According to Colossians 2:12, the phrase "be risen with Christ" refers to someone who has been raised from the dead. The phrase "be risen with Christ" is not a poetic or figurative term. Before people are saved they are not kind of dead, or mostly dead. Instead, before people are saved they are just as dead as people in a cemetery. However, after they are saved they are alive. So this phrase refers to an actual resurrection from the dead.

Since believers have the same body they had before they were saved, they must have been raised in their spiritual part, in their souls. Although not visible to the human eye, the resurrection of their souls is just as real as a physical resurrection. That is, before they were saved, Christians were really dead in sin (Eph. 2:1, Col. 2:13). Furthermore, they died the death of the wrath of God in punishment for sin. They did not endure that wrath personally, but in the sense that Jesus represented them when He paid for their sins. Nevertheless, before they were saved, Christians were just as dead as Christ was, who paid the penalty of death for their sins (Isaiah 53:5, Rom. 6:3-4, Col. 1:14,22). After they are saved, Christians have life (John 5:24, Col. 2:13). Therefore being "risen" is a real from-death-to-life experience, even though it is a spiritual experience.

The words, "with Christ," link the reality of believers' resurrection to Jesus' own resurrection (Eph. 2:6, Col. 2:13). Believers were as dead as Christ was, who paid the penalty of death for their sins. Believers were raised from that death as Christ was, who now reigns over all (Eph. 1:19-21, Phil. 2:9,10).

Altogether, the phrase, "be risen with Christ," means to be saved by the grace of God, which includes not only what God does **for** His people judicially in paying for sins, but also what God does **to** His people in bestowing upon them a new life. So the intent of the phrase, "if ye then be risen with Christ," can be expressed as, "If you are saved, I have some advice to help you deal with your sins."

With all of this in mind, we can say that a more complete title for Colossians 3 would be God's program for dealing with sin **in a Christian's life**. That is, the counsel of this chapter is meant exclusively for Christians. **Only** Christians want the advice and **all** Christians have the power to apply it to their lives. We do not imply that Colossians 3 has no message for unbelievers. God uses all of His Word to deal with them, too. After all, God uses His Word to call to salvation all those whom He intends to save (Rom. 10:17, I Peter 2:23). As long as someone is physically alive, there is hope. So, God can use the opening "if" statement of Colossians 3 to graciously call people into His Kingdom. Furthermore, God uses His Word to prepare for judgment all those who refuse to submit to His will (John 3:19, 12:48). Nevertheless, when we think of Colossians 3 as a guide to help people gain victory over sin, then we must understand that it is intended for believers.

The word "seek" is a word of action. We find it translated in Acts 21:31, "went about." This word is in a grammatical form that indicates a command. It is a command given with the expectation that a person who is "risen with Christ" will obey. From this we have one of two fundamental principles which form the foundation of God's plan for gaining victory over sin. As we stated before we began our analysis of verse 1, the first principle is that a true, born again believer **can** obey and turn from his sin.

Colossians 3:1 teaches that a believer can walk obediently because he has been raised to a new life in Christ and has the greater power of the resurrected life within him (II Cor. 5:15, Phil. 2:12,13, Col. 2:12,13, Gal. 2:20, I John 4:4). He does not have to sin (Rom. 8:12-13). If a man is saved God rules in his heart (Col. 3:15) and the power of sin does not dominant him.

One conclusion we can make is that when a believer sins he realizes he can blame only himself (James 1:14). For one thing, a believer does not react to the discovery of his own sin with alibis, rationalizations, or excuses. Instead, he cries out in sorrow (Psalm 32:5, 51:3). His wickedness defiles and fights against his new nature (Gal. 5:17). Also, his sin is a grief to him because his wickedness saddens and dishonors God, who has shown him so much love in the Gospel (Luke 22:62). For another thing, a believer recognizes that while he may be born with a particular strong sin tendency, peculiar to his own personality, he does not have to indulge it. Instead, he recognizes God knows his weakness better than he (Psalm 103:14), and that he must not neglect the divine wisdom and power available to him (Phil. 4:13,19, Jude 24).

Another conclusion we can make is that a person who continues unsuccessfully to struggle with his sin must take the constant defeat seriously, especially in light of the power that is available to someone who is "raised from the dead." A person whose life is dominated by a particular sin must not casually think, "I made a profession of faith" or "I am a member of the church, therefore I am saved, even though I happen to be living like the world." Rather, a person must seriously think, "No matter what I said or did outwardly in the past, if I continue to live like the world, am I really saved?" A true believer can seek the things above, so no evidence of seeking means no evidence of salvation.

The word "seek" is a word of action with a purpose or objective, described as "those things which are above." So, dealing successfully with sin requires a heavenly goal and a heavenly focus in the business of daily life. It is not true that to be heavenly minded is to be of no earthly good, as if someone who is always thinking of Heaven is incapable of being any use for the practical affairs of daily living on earth. In fact, the only way to be of any earthly good is to be heavenly minded. There is nothing more practical than salvation and God's momentary aid in a person's daily struggle with sin.

The words, "seek ... above" remind us of prayer. That vital ingredient in gaining victory over against sin and temptation will be discussed later when we look at the phrase, "and be ye thankful," found in verse 15. For now we can say that they highlight the heavenly, prayerful focus that victory requires.

The words, "where Christ sitteth on the right hand of God," do not mean Jesus sits in repose, detached from the affairs of His people. Rather, the "right hand" of God is the place of supreme authority (Eph. 1:20,21). Jesus sits and reigns with supreme authority as the Creator (Col. 1:16) and as the Redeemer of His church (Col. 1:18). Since Jesus sits on the right hand of God, He rules with sufficient authority to cause His people to deal successfully with their sin. They no longer owe obedience to sin (Rom. 8:12), for it is no longer their master (Rom. 6:17,18). Jesus is. Sin has no overwhelming control over them. Jesus does. Therefore, the command to "seek" is accompanied by the authority and power of God to help fulfill that command. That is why the first principle is true. With that in mind, the issue of dealing with sin comes down to the question of, "Who is your Lord and Master?" That is, "Are you saved and so is Jesus your Lord? Or are you unsaved and under the authority of your own sinful desires and Satan's influence?" (Rom. 6:16)

In addition to that, according to Ephesians 2:6, people who have been "risen with Christ" sit where Jesus does. They rule with authority, too, as the Bible states, "as kings" (Rev. 1:6). It is not that they are rivals to Jesus' authority or that they have jurisdiction in a part of the universe that is equal to or exceeds Jesus' authority in some way. Instead, their authority is expressed in different ways, two of which are as follows. When Christians bring the Bible's message of the Gospel, not only is what they say backed by the authority of God Himself, but also God works through their testimony to save some people and prepare others for judgment (II Cor. 2:15-16, 5:20). Also, Christians rule over their own sinful flesh (Rom. 6:12-14). God's resurrection power within them enables the desires of their soul to reign over the desires of their flesh, so that they can live obediently (Rom. 5:17,21).

We must remember that the reason believers are successful in their struggle with sin is that they do not fight the battle themselves. God fights for and in them. Their victory is based upon Jesus' personal victory over sin and death in His sacrifice before the law, together with

His abiding work in their hearts. That victory is seen at the present time in Christians' ability to walk after the Spirit (Rom. 8:1-5, Gal. 5:25), and will be revealed at the end of time in the renewal of the universe, which includes believers' bodies, too. Again, the principle is that believers **can** seek the will of God.

Colossians 3:2, "Set your affection on things above, not on things on the earth."

The second of two fundamental principles that form the foundation of God's plan for gaining victory over sin is:

A true born again believer **wants to** turn from sin and obey God.

Now let us look at the details of verse 2 that lead up to and support this principle.

The word "affection," used in the King James Bible, is really the word "mind." At this point, we have to be careful. The counsel of this verse is not that we can meditate our way out of sin and temptation. God's plan is not "mind over matter," at least not man's mind. Nor can we say that accurate thinking based upon correct knowledge is enough to assure victory over sin. A good education simply makes educated sinners. Rather, the idea is that God works through the minds of His people by His power so that they do His will (Rom. 12:2, I Cor. 2:16, Phil 4:6-9). That is why, as we shall see, the counsel of Colossians 3:16 is so important.

Even though the Greek word is properly "mind," the word "affection" is quite appropriate because a man thinks about those things for which he has an affection. An unsaved man loves this world. For him Heaven is so remote, if he thinks that it exists at all. Besides, the exciting physical universe is a good place to hide or cover up the guilt that he feels. So an unsaved person has given his heart to the world and sets his mind upon its charms. A believer is also part of this world, at least in his body. But, unlike an unbeliever, he is not of this world (John 15:19). He is really a citizen of a different world (Phil. 3:20, Col. 1:13). He really wants to do the will of his heavenly Master. His heart has been captured by Jesus and his mind is full of His words, which he dearly wants to obey. The focus of a believer's mind and heart is upon his Lord who is sitting enthroned in Heaven, not in leisure but in control. From this we have the second of two fundamental principles which form the foundation of God's plan for gaining victory over sin. As we stated above, the second principle is that a true, born again believer **wants to** obey and does not really want to sin.

It is true that sin is attractive to a believer's flesh, which has not yet been changed (Rom. 7:18-24). So, in a superficial way, he does want to sin. A believer is aware that it is easy to develop an affection and appetite for sin. Sin is fun and delicious, for a while, even when a person realizes the bitter fruit of misery that it produces (Rom. 6:21). Yet when a believer does sin, his reaction is quite unlike that of an unbeliever who tries to justify himself. A believer cannot continue in his sin. It violates his new nature. Deep in his heart and soul he does not want to sin. So, after he sins, he reacts in brokenness and sorrow (Psalm 51:4, II Cor. 7:10). A believer is honest about his situation and has a heart that earnestly seeks to turn from his sin and please God.

A person's desire, or "want to," is the seat of sin. For as we saw in Chapter 2 of this book, sin is a matter of the will (Col. 3:24). Maybe for a short time one person can force another person to do outwardly what the Bible commands. However, no one can make another person want to do God's will, no one can except God Himself. Only God can change a person's "want to," or rather exchange it. Only God can replace a sinner's old heart and its affections with a new heart and its affections (Ezek. 36:25,26). That is why salvation is the only hope for dealing with sin. The Gospel alone has the power for salvation and the power to help people set their affection on things above. That heavenly desire is a big witness to the fact that they are "risen with Christ." That desire is a big witness to the fact that God indeed has worked and continues to work in their lives with resurrection power.

The focus of Colossians 3:2 is upon the mind because that is the factory of sin. That is where sin begins and where the battle must be won. Let us trace the way of sin in our minds. When a sinful thought comes into our minds, the tendency of our flesh is to focus and dwell upon it. For example, sometimes we fondle our sin thinking that a little taste is all we need at the moment. We turn it over in our minds and it grows bigger and bigger, soon dominating almost every waking moment of our day. We feel sorry for ourselves when we have an affection for something and cannot have what we yearn. We are afraid of losing it. We feel deprived of something special and want it in contradiction to God's will. The next step is capitulation, no matter what God says. In another example, sometimes we foolishly think we are in control and try to "figure out" our sin. We try to "better understand" it by analyzing it in order to get rid of it. At that point we are ripe for surrendering to it. The message of Colossians is that we must not think about it at all. We must think about things above. We are not so in control of the situation or of ourselves. We must flee such thoughts the moment they come to our minds and, as this verse says, turn the focus of our attention upon God.

Sin is strong, so very strong! We must realize how strong sin is. We must realize how strong our desire to sin is. We must realize how strongly attracted to sin we fallen humans are. Sin is stronger that we are. That is, our attraction to sin is stronger than our own power to resist it effectively. But God is stronger than sin. God is not attracted to sin but He is powerful enough to keep us from falling into sin. According to Colossians 3:1,2, if we are saved, **we can** and **want to** exercise the power of the resurrected life, beginning with our minds. As we fill our minds with and meditate upon the things above, we will reveal the work of God within us and gain the peace at heart which is a testimony to ourselves and others that we are "risen with Christ" (II Cor. 10:5, Phil. 2:12,13).

A summary of verses 1 and 2

Before we continue with a brief examination of the following verses, it would be good to summarize the main ideas of verses 1 and 2. Colossians 3:1 and 2 are like two thesis statements. They state two principles which are developed in the rest of the chapter. The first principle can be stated in this way: People who have been "raised with Christ" do not **have to** sin. They can obey their Lord. Colossians 3:2 states the second principle: People who have been "raised with Christ" do not **want to** sin. They have a holy affection for the things above which is greater than their sinful affection for the things of this world.

A few important companion ideas

We now are ready to make some important observations about the struggle Christians have with their sins. These observations will help us understand the foundation upon which God builds His program for gaining victory over His peoples' sins and the tactics He prescribes for fulfilling that program in their lives.

a. Salvation is the foundation for gaining victory over sin

Based upon the phrase "be risen with Christ," we can state that salvation is the foundation for gaining victory over sin. We can understand this observation in two ways.

First of all, salvation is the foundation for gaining victory over sin in the sense that people first must be saved in order to deal successfully with it (Rom. 8:1-4). For people who are not Christians, successfully dealing with sin begins with seeking the mercy and grace of God for salvation. For Christians, the first step in dealing with sin is to "make sure that you are saved!"

As we face the so-called "practical" issue of dealing with sin, we must keep in mind that there is no separation between the doctrines of salvation and advice for Christian life. Truth in one leads to truth in the another. Error in one leads to error in the other. A person who does not correctly understand the doctrines of grace will eventually show it by how he lives his life. Conversely, any sin of attitude or behavior to which a person clings will eventually affect his understanding of salvation. That is why the best basis for a faithful walk with God is a correct understanding of salvation. Similarly, only a person with a humble willingness to submit to God's commands for his life is open to the truths of salvation as presented in the Bible.

Maybe we can better understand the idea that salvation is the basis for gaining victory over sin by asking the following questions. Is God's counsel, "Let me tell you how to do a better job than Adam and Eve"? Does God point us in the right direction and send us off to just try harder? Is our task to copy Jesus' life more carefully? Is the key to solving our sin problem leading a good life and going to church? Does a sincere effort count? The answer to all of these questions is, "No." Anyone who seeks to take the necessary steps to gain victory over the sins in his life, must understand that Colossians 3, or any part of the Bible for that matter, is not a do-it-yourself kit. As we said, dealing with our sins is really a salvation issue.

People who are not saved have no interest in denying their sinful desires and have no ability to turn from their sin, even if they wanted to. However, people who are saved have the desire and power to turn from their sin. Jesus Christ has given them a new life. They are animated by new motivations, objectives and abilities. Therefore, gaining victory over sin is first of all not a moral issue of performance, but an issue of salvation. Dealing with sin begins with redemption, which is a rescue from the wrath of God, and is accompanied by the resurrecting power of the Gospel. The expected moral and spiritual virtues that attend salvation are the resulting fruits, not the initial objective of the Gospel.

The answer to the question, "What can I do about my sins?" is "You can do nothing about it yourself." One reason is that we have accumulated a record of disobedience, for which we are accountable, that we are not able to erase by our own efforts. An inventory of our sins is not a list of wrong or neglected actions which we simply need to properly complete in order to fulfill our obligation. In other words, solving our sin problem is not just a matter of eventually finishing what we were supposed to do. Nor is solving our sin problem a matter of adding acts of obedience to our record that hopefully will balance out or compensate for our acts of disobedience. The answer to the question "What can I do about my sins?" never is "Do better next time" or "Try to redo the job and fix what you did wrong in order to make up the difference for your mistake" or "Be good so your deeds will out weigh or cancel your bad behavior." No one can start life again with a clean slate. No one can go back, erase, and correct his acts of wilful disobedience. Every sin is a permanent, indelible mark in the book that God will open on Judgment Day in order to confirm the frightful destiny of every unsaved sinner (Rev. 20:12).

Another reason the answer is "You can do nothing about it yourself" is that we can do nothing in our own wisdom and strength. When God first meets us, we are dead. Turning from our sin and obeying God are impossible tasks (Matt. 19:26, Mark 10:27, Luke 18:27). We cannot raise ourselves from the dead. But what is impossible with man is possible with God. Only God can remove the judicial barrier between a sinner and His grace, and only God can raise up that which is dead.

As we explained in Chapter 2, our sin problem is really God's problem to solve. He first removes the penalty and power of sin through the sacrifice of Jesus. He then continues to deal with sin in the lives of His people after they are saved. It is all of God. Therefore, victory over sin begins by heeding the warning, "be sure that you are saved!"

In addition to that, salvation is the foundation for gaining victory over sin in the sense that after people are saved they must apply the same principles to their sin problem that brought them salvation in the first place. As we read in Colossians 2:6, Christians walk in Christ the same way they receive Him. Let us examine the process or means though which God saves people in order to understand how to gain victory over our sins.

We begin with the fact that God causes people whom He saves to recognize and focus upon their own personal sins (Psalm 32:5, 38:18, Prov. 28:13, I John 1:8,9). That is, in any situation that might lead Christians into sin or in which they have sinned, they must focus upon their own sin problem and not on the sins of another person, as real and as aggravating as the other person's sins may be. In any situation, especially when their sin involves a conflict with another person, they must contritely recognize their own culpability. They must face the shame associated with their own sin as well as be aware of the consequences they deserve, whether they are spared those consequences or not. That personal focus will make their sin problem clearer in their minds and make their struggle with sin less complicated.

Next, we turn to the fact that God causes people whom He saves to trust Him (Phil. 1:29). In any situation that might lead Christians to sin or in which they have sinned, they must believe the promise of His grace, trusting that He will forgive according to His Word. Also, they must trust His control over all things in their daily lives. For example, when their carefully prepared plans fall apart, when they are arrested from attaining something they want, or when they wonder about an unfair situation, they must not impatiently and aggressively strive to achieve what they want through their own wisdom and strength. Neither must they compare their situation with that of another person and become jealous, frustrated, bitter or vengeful. Rather, they must trust that God is always in control and can change any situation as He sees fit. They must conclude that things are the way they are because God has allowed them to be so. Then they must abandon themselves to God's management over the affairs of each day, expecting that God's ways are best and that He will direct things for their good and His glory. They must trust that no situation is more than God can handle. No situation can prevent Him from doing His good and perfect will.

Associated with the need to trust in God is the principle that people cannot serve two masters (Matt. 6:24). In addition to trusting God, people who seek to deal with sin must simultaneously relinquish control of the things that they treasure (Phil 3:13). They must give all those things to God. They must abandon all of own their plans, jealousies, resentments, hurts, fears, desires, or anything else that would divide their loyalty and keep them anchored to this world. On one hand, people who trust God must understand that God means what He says when He threatens to destroy all idols, together with the people who cling to them (I Cor. 6:13). On the other hand, people who trust God must delight more in the Lord than in any earthly pleasures or treasures. The things of this world, which includes the desires of their flesh, work against their efforts to gain victory over their sin and their efforts to serve God whom they claim to love (Gal. 5:17). Therefore, anyone who trusts God in a half-hearted, double-minded way will never receive victory over his sin (James 1:6-8).

Finally, we face the fact that God causes people whom He saves to take deliberate steps of contrite repentance (Psalm 37:23, 143:8). In any situation that might lead Christians into sin or in which they have sinned, they must never think that a little indulgence does not matter or that they can take care of their sin sometime later. Sin problems only get worse. Sloth in this area often leads to great sorrow later. In fact, some people's procrastination may be an indication that they have no interest in God's will because He really is not their Lord and Savior, even though they might think He is. On the other hand, a true believer can take and wants to take prompt steps to change his attitude and pattern of behavior.

We can conclude our observation that salvation is the basis for dealing with sin by looking at I Corinthians 10:17. According to I Corinthians 10:17, God makes a "way to escape" for people who face sins and temptations. The word translated "way to escape" is used only twice in the Bible, once in I Corinthians and once in Hebrews 13:7 as "end." In Hebrews, it refers to the faithful lifestyle of rulers, whose way the other members should follow. The word translated "way to escape" is a combination of the prefix "away from" and the root, "feet." The root is used only in Acts 3:7, to refer to a man's restored feet as a picture of salvation. Our conclusion from all of this is that I Corinthians 10:17 teaches we have a "way to escape" only if God has given us "feet" to walk "away from" the sins and temptations. Those are feet that accompany salvation. The point is that a Christian's ability to deal successfully with sins and temptations begins with and continues all his life by God's work of grace (II Peter 3:18).

b. A finished work of God

Being "raised with Christ" does not mean people are raised part way or raised by installments. Salvation is an all-or-nothing proposition. In terms of John 15, a person either abides in the vine and produces fruit or he does not produce fruit because he is not in the vine. The fact is that the Holy Spirit fully equips a Christian to deal with sin (Rom. 8:13,14).

Since God's work of salvation is something that He does without any participation by those who are saved, it is a perfect and complete work that needs no amendments. Therefore, a Christian's objective for gaining victory over sin is not to prepare himself for entrance into Heaven. Colossians 3 is not a plan to help him be good enough to be accepted by God or to allow him to fix something in his life before he meets God. The notion that gaining victory over sin is a clean-up in preparation for entering Heaven implies that Jesus' atonement was insufficient, and that something is missing which is supplied by our own works or the work of someone else on our behalf. However, Jesus alone made full access to the Father for all of His children, inasmuch as he disposed of the barrier to Heaven that their sins erected. That access is available, both now in prayer (Eph. 2:18, Heb. 4:16) and after death when Christians go to be with God (Phil. 1:21-23). That is both a relief and a caution. It is a relief for Christians who understand that their right to enter Heaven is independent of their uncertain efforts in dealing with sin, and a caution for people who think that it is not.

c. Christians still sin

Colossians 3 is addressed to people who are "risen with Christ." The idea is that the counsel of the chapter is meant for Christians because they need it. The implication is that Christians sin. Do people who have the heart and the power to do God's will still sin? Yes. That is what God teaches in Romans 7:18-25. Keeping that fact in mind helps Christians deal with their sin.

First of all, the recognition that Christians do sin arrests any tendency to pride. The message is, "Don't think that you are perfect, super holy and without sin. That is a conceit and a deceit that fools no one but yourself" (I John 1:8). Christians must never attempt to protect their pride and self-respect because that action would be a barrier to gaining victory over sin. Christians must be humbly honest about themselves and their need of God's help. Their souls are righteous, the proof of which is that the moment they die they go to Heaven in the presence of a Holy God (II Cor. 5:8). However, while on earth, they are in a sinful body that continues to delight in its own sinful desires (Rom. 7:17-20).

Secondly, the recognition that Christians do sin provides solace in their struggle. The message is, "When you sin don't be overly discouraged or fearful." It is important to understand that the presence of sin in a person's life is not an indication of a loss of salvation. It is a reminder of the fact that after a person is saved, he is a walking civil war (Rom. 7:23). This is both an encouraging and a sobering fact.

A person is encouraged by the fact that he struggles because the battle shows he has life within him. We can compare this to a fish in the water. A dead fish is swept along with the prevailing tides and currents. But a fish that is alive often swims and struggles against them. Similarly, a Christian's struggles against sin is good news because those struggles reveal he is a true Christian, that he is spiritually alive. If he were still spiritually dead, he would conform to the desires of his flesh without an intense or prolonged conflict. But since he is alive, he has both the desire and ability to fight against his flesh.

A Christian must keep in mind that a person who is saved can never lose his eternal salvation (John 10:27-29, Rom. 6:23, Eph. 1:13). He can trust God's promise to keep him (Phil. 1:6, II Tim. 1:12). Although sin is found in his life, repentance and faith will follow, because he really is saved. That realization should drive him to seek the wisdom and power of God he needs to turn from his sin. And as time goes by, he will gain victory over this sin and that sin, never completing the job but always showing evidence of striving to be more faithful (Phil 3:13,14).

Thirdly, the recognition that Christians do sin provides the encouragement of companionship, for the word "ye" is a plural pronoun that embraces many people. The message is, "Don't think that you are the only one who is struggling with sin. You aren't weird or especially wicked." That is, not only does a Christian still sin, but all his brethren do too. It is not that a Christian is happy that other Christians agonize over their sins. Rather, the struggles he observes in other people's lives reinforce the thought that God has not abandoned him and that he must not be weary in well doing, but press on.

Finally, a person is sobered by the fact that he continues to struggle with a particular sin because a besetting sin could be an indication that the sin is par for the course in his life, that the sin is dominant and in control, that he is really not saved and has never been saved, despite his outward claim. That realization should drive him to seek the salvation of the Bible. When a person sins, it is always appropriate for him to reassess his spiritual condition and ask "Am I truly saved?" (II Cor. 13:5) If he really is saved, then he will be assured of his salvation by the Word of God (Rom. 8:16, 10:17). But he should never be so surprised at the wicked things he says and does. After all, what else is new? What does he expect, especially when he remembers that He is still encumbered by a body infected with sin? The issue is not whether a Christian sins, but "what does he do after?" Colossians 3 explains what should come after, if a person is truly raised with Christ.

Incidentally, the words, "Whosoever is born of God doth not commit sin; for his seed remaineth in him: and he cannot sin, because he is born of God," found in I John 3:9 do not contradict our claim that Christians still sin. In fact, the book of 1 John itself states, "If we say that we have no sin, we deceive ourselves, and the truth is not in us" (I John 1:8). I John 3:9 refers to the "inward man" which delights in the law of God (Rom. 7:22). A person who is saved is perfect in his soul. We say that based upon statement that, after a Christian dies, he goes directly to God's Holy heaven without any intervening purification (II Cor. 5:8).

d. Why do Christians sin?

The Bible teaches, which our own experience supports, that Christians sin because they still live in their sin-corrupted bodies (Rom. 7:17-19). However, at this point we could ask, "Why would God allow Christians to sin, especially when we think about the great problem it is for them? Couldn't God prevent them from sinning? Doesn't I John 4:4 state that God is stronger than sin and Satan?" Yes, God could prevent Christians from committing many of the sins they do. The fact is that He does restrain sin in their lives, much more than in unbelievers' lives. In fact, it is only because of God's power that anyone turns from sin and obeys Him at all. Nevertheless, God does not prevent every sin. He allows some sins to continue in the lives of His people until the day they die. Is there any possible reason for that?

We do not know all that God knows or intends to do through the affairs of men, including the lives of His people. But some things are easy to understand. One reason God allows sin to persist in Christians' lives is that it teaches them something about God. They learn that when he does prevent any sin it is because He is so gracious and kind to people so undeserving (Psalm 107:9-13).

A second reason God allows sin to persist in Christians' lives is that it teaches them something about themselves. Christians' sins humble them as their sins force them to have a realistic self-image. Their sins remind them of their personal sin-tendencies and highlights their dependence upon God's abiding care (Rom. 7:24,25).

A third reason God allows sin to persist in Christians' lives is that it teaches them something about the Gospel. As Christians eventually gain victory over particular sins, they see that the promises and power of God's Gospel are real (Titus 3:3-6).

A fourth reason God allows sin to persist in Christians' lives is that it teaches them something about other people. On one hand, they observe other people struggling with a common foe, and are reminded that all people are earthen vessels, weak and in need of patience and mercy (II Tim. 2:22-25). It causes Christians to be sensitive and sympathetic with other people. They learn that other people should be targets of Gospel comfort, rather than criticism. On the other hand, as Christians slowly over time grow in spiritual strength, they become wise to the wiles of the world and the spiritual attacks of their enemies. So it causes Christians to have a realistic image of other people, and to trust God rather than men (Psalm 108:12).

e. Christians are victorious

In Colossians 1:3-6 we read, "we thank God ... since we heard of your faith ... and bringeth forth fruit, as it doth also in you." The fact is that Christians do eventually gain victory over a sin with which they are struggling (Col. 1:10, 2:5). That is what we read in Romans 8:1-5.

The realistic message of Romans 7, that Christians struggle in this world with the sins that so easily beset them, is followed by the message of Romans 8, that Christians do gain victory over sins. That victory is the hallmark of a true Christian's life. Even if, as Romans 7 points out, Christians temporarily lose some battles with a particular sin, they always win the war, because that sin cannot determine their eternal destiny, nor can it continue to determine their behavior. The point is that when a Christian submits to God's plan, there is a real expectation of success.

However, victory over sin is not a testimony to Christians' personal diligence and valor. God does not design a wise plan to overcome sin, disclose it to Christians, then equip them to gain the victory independently by their own earnest efforts. Rather, the victory is God's (Rom. 8:37, I Cor.15:57, II Cor. 2:14). It is God's victory in the sense that He has done all that is necessary in Jesus' atonement to vanquish His peoples' sin. And it is God's victory in the sense that He is the one who animates His people to deal with their sin (Gal. 2:20, Phil. 2:13).

Also, victory over sin does not mean that the propensity to fall into the same sin has been totally eliminated or that Christians will never sin in a particular way again. Instead, the victory is in the sense that, as time goes by, Christians grow and are more and more successful in recognizing and avoiding a particular sin that God brings to their attention. That is, Christians learn to depend more and more upon the wisdom and power of God in different situations (Prov. 3:5,6), recognizing that though they are weak, He remains faithful (II Tim. 2:13).

From that point of view, we could say that Colossians 3 presents two strong evidences that a person is a true believer. That is, if his greatest desire is to serve God and not himself, and if he reveals the power to gain victories over sins, then he reveals that he is indeed saved, and is under the authority of God.

f. Vigilance is required

Hebrews 12:2 warns that we must be aware of "the sin which doth so easily beset us." Sin is handy. It is as nearby as our flesh. The potential for becoming entangled in sin exists in every life situation. Therefore, the struggle against sin is a 24-hour-a-day job. Also, it continues until the day Christians die. The message is Christians must recognize that the struggle against their sin requires that they constantly be watchful. It can be expressed as, "Don't think you can let down your guard."

For example, Christians must understand that even though, by God's grace and abiding power, they have resisted the attractions of a particular sin for a time, that sin and its appeal never completely disappears. They must ever watch lest they once more heed and answer its appeal to their flesh. In another example, while God in His wisdom removes some issues of sin early in Christians' lives, He allows many others to remain so that they must deal with them, one at a time, over the remainder of their lives on this earth. That is, when God gives them victory over a particular sin, another sin that they had not previously noticed soon demands their attention. So they must begin to work on it. And yet each victory gives them wisdom to effectively struggle with the next sin, as well as confidence in God, who used His power to help them deal successfully with their past sins.

Christians must be diligent in Bible study and prayer in order to be prepared to deal with the temptations to sin they face every moment. Only through those two means will Christians have the wisdom and power to remain constantly vigilant, which is part of their struggle with sin as long as they live on this earth.

Now, let us resume our analysis of Colossians 3. The remaining verses give us a deeper insight into the two principles found in verses 1 and 2.

Colossians 3:3, "For ye are dead, and your life is hid with Christ in God."

This verse gives the reason why the principles stated in verses 1 and 2 are true. Christians are able to gain victory over their sins because they are "dead." At this point, we must make sure that we understand what is in view when the Bible uses the word "dead." The word can refer to at least three different but closely related ideas.

One death is physical death (Eccl. 12:7). That is a death which is experienced by all men, both unsaved and saved, except for those people who are physically alive when Jesus returns to conclude history on earth. That is not the kind of death in view here because the Colossian readers were still physically alive, as are all who read these words today.

Another death is spiritual death of the soul (Col. 2:13). That death also is shared by all men, but is the death from which God's people are resurrected when they become saved, and is the death in which all unsaved people remain eternally. That, also, is not the kind of death meant in verse 3 because the word "dead" is applied to believers' present situation. Believers were dead in their souls before they were saved, but they are no longer dead in that way.

Still one more death is the death in Hell. It is referred to in the Bible as the "second death" (Rev. 2:11, 20:6, 21:8) because it is an event that follows the 'first death,' namely physical death (Heb. 9:27). It is the payment required for sins, which is eternally enduring the wrath of God. In other words, it is the death that accompanies condemnation. The death associated with God's wrath is also shared by all men. However, that is the death that saved people experience differently from those who are never saved. Those who are saved experience it in Jesus, since He died for them, while all who are not saved will experience that death on the their own. This is the death upon which Colossians 3:3 focuses.

The death in view is the death that believers experience as part of the salvation work of Jesus. That is, when Jesus died He took their sins with Him and so in effect they died, too (Col. 2:12). But more than a judicial compensation, more than fulfilling the command that the "the soul that sinneth, it shall die" (Ezek. 18:4, Rom. 6:23), Jesus' death also was a release. That is the implication of the prefix "away from" which is attached to the front of the word translated “dead” in Colossians 3:3. Those who are “risen with Christ” no longer obey their former master because they have been set free from that master and belong to a new Master (Col. 1:13).

Now that we have a clearer view of the word “dead,” let us try to understand the message of Colossians 3:3. We shall begin by thinking of people as beings who are created in two parts, body and soul. Because of the sin of Adam, all people inherit a dead soul and a body full of sin. Since they have no life in their souls, unsaved people are dominated by the sin in their bodies. The lusts of their bodies draw unsaved people into sin, unimpeded by any resistance to sin which would come from their souls, which are dead. The Gospel changes that situation.

One result of the Gospel is that believers are “dead” with Christ. The simplest way to think about this is that death separates people from their bodies. People who become believers do not die physically, but the separation of believers from their bodies is just as real. This is important because it means believers are separated from the sin that is in their bodies in the sense that sin no longer has dominion over them. That is why Romans 6:2 states that they are dead "to sin," rather than dead to their bodies.

Another result of the Gospel is that believers are “risen with Christ.” (Col. 3:1). The simplest way to think about this is that believers’ souls are no longer dead but alive. They have experienced a spiritual resurrection in their souls. People who become believers have a new life, not a restored life in the image of Adam, but an eternal life, a life described in both Romans 5 and 6 as Jesus’ own life. The life they have is not an independent life of their own. It is the life of Jesus Himself who is within them (John 14:6, Gal. 2:20, Col. 1:27). It is eternal life, not just in the sense that it is life without end, but especially in the sense that it is the life of the eternal God. That is, eternal life is a statement of quality as much as it is of duration. This is important because it means believers, who continue to live in their sinful bodies until they die physically or until the Lord returns, now have the power of Jesus’ life in their souls that enables them to resist the pull of the sinful desires in their bodies. They both can and want to do God’s will.

Therefore, the reason the principles stated in Colossians 3:1-2 are true is that Christians have died to sin, or rather to the power of sin, and have the greater power of the resurrected life within them (Col. 2:12,20). Again, they both **can** and **want to** do God’s will.

Colossians 3:3, adds that believers are "hid with Christ in God." The word "hid" is used to highlight the fact that the blessings of a new resurrected life are not recognized or understood by unbelievers (II Cor. 4:3). The whole idea of dealing with sin makes no sense to people who are not saved. Anyone who willingly denies himself the pleasures of sin in order to serve God is strange in the eyes of unbelievers (I Peter 4:3,4), and is either pitied or mocked by them.

Colossians 3:4, "When Christ, who is our life, shall appear, then shall ye also appear with him in glory."

This verse states the objective of the two principles given in verses 1 and 2. The objective is that when Jesus Christ "shall appear, ... then shall ye (Christians) also appear with him in glory." How is that important in Christians' struggles against their sins?

For one thing, verse 4 promises that Jesus shall indeed "appear." That means believers will not struggle with their sins forever. Jesus will return to remove this sin-cursed world and replace it with a new incorruptible one (II Peter 3:13), which includes Christians' glorified spiritual bodies (I Cor. 15:42-44). So, their struggles with sins will eventually end in complete victory. Christians will be given victory in the sense that they will be free from the present demands of their sinful flesh, which annoys and grieves them. They also will be given victory in the sense that they will be free to honor and praise God perfectly, as He deserves, and they yearn to do, without the impediments and blemishes of sinful motives and actions. But for now, they must keep their focus on things above, as they deal with sin here on earth.

The present victories which Christians experience in this corrupt material world show that their hope in the future appearance of Jesus is not misplaced or some "hope-so," "pie-in-the-sky-by-and-by" mental invention. Their present victories over their sins are witnesses to the reality of God's promises and power, for anyone who has eyes to see. Jesus' future appearance is as real as His power to give them present victories over their sins. Christians must not faint or grow weary in their struggles with their sins. The struggles are abiding, wearing and a source of sorrow for now, but the promised end is in sight and makes the struggles worthwhile (II Cor. 4:16-18).

In addition to that, when Jesus appears, Christians will "appear with him in glory." It is not that by gaining victory over sin, Christians earn the right to appear with Jesus in glory. Rather it is that, thinking back to verse 3, the victory reveals that their "life is hid with Christ in God," that they have been "risen with Christ." When Jesus appears, Christians will not be separated from Him as guilty criminals. Instead, they will be with Him as dear children, sharing the blessings of His grace. They are people who have been made ready by God's grace to meet Jesus inasmuch as they are in God as a shelter, hidden from the judgment that will come when Christ appears (Psalm 27:5, 32:7, 90:1, Rom 8:1).

Struggle with sin and assurance of salvation

When a verse such as Colossians 3:4 reminds people of the appearance of Christ, there are two possible reactions in their hearts. One is joy (Jude 24) and another is fear (Rev. 6:16). The reactions are based upon whether a person is saved or not.

It is a wonder that Jesus came to earth the first time to save His people from their sins. That work provided a certain and eternally secure salvation, that no one can erode or reverse. To that we can add another wonder, namely, believers can be absolutely sure they are saved. In other words, not only can believers know that God's salvation is true, but also they can know it is true for them. That personal conviction is called assurance.

God's people are not left to question if their Christian experience is a mental or emotional illusion. The message of the Bible is that "we know" (I John 4:13, 5:13). The assurance God's people have is based upon facts. They have evidence that they have been transformed by God's grace. According to Colossians 3:1 and 2, the evidence is that they can and want to obey their Lord. How is this evidence seen? The book of I John lists some of the ways. God's people have dealt with their sins in Christ (I John 1:9, 2:12) and continue to live faithful, obedient lives (I John 2:3,5,29). They are able to recognize and endure spiritual attacks (I John 4:4, 5:18). They genuinely love their brothers (I John 3:14,18,19). And they have the Spirit within them, Who bears witness with their spirits that they indeed are the children of God (Rom. 8:16).

Every person struggles with his own personal sin problems. Those struggles can cause him to question his spiritual situation. If discouragement and doubt dominate a person, if fear persistently lingers in his heart, then it is appropriate for him to ask, "Why do I fear? Is it because I am not saved?"

A true believer can draw upon those things he has close at hand in order to keep his thinking straight about his own spiritual situation. A list of those resources includes the true propositional statements of the Bible, prayer, and his past record of obedience amid temptations, as imperfect as that record is. With the evidence in place that he is saved, he can welcome the promise that "Christ ... shall appear." A person who is assured that God loves him as His child has inner peace, boldness before God and courage before men.

Now let us turn to Colossians 3:5-9. These verses develop the first principle. They show how the power of the resurrected life within believers overcomes the power of sin in their members so that they can obey. They **do not have to** sin (Rom. 8:12).

Colossians 3:5, "Mortify therefore your members which are upon the earth; fornication, uncleanness, inordinate affection, evil concupiscence, and covetousness, which is idolatry:"

The word translated "mortify" in verse 5 means to put to death. The word "members" refers to the residence of sin, a person's body of flesh (Rom. 7:18,23). The counsel is that Christians who seek to gain victory over sin must kill their members (Gal. 5:24). There is no easy way out. We cannot escape this procedure. God expects His people to mortify their members.

This verse does not promote physical mutilation (c.f. Matt. 5:29,30). Besides, that would not help anyone refrain from sin. Only complete physical death would. Nor is this verse a call to suicide, which is self-murder. Interestingly, in the other two places where this form of the Greek word is used, namely the one translated "mortify," it does not actually refer to physical death. Instead, the idea can be expressed as "a body that is alive but unable to function, as if it were dead" (Rom. 4:19, Heb. 11:12). To deny a sinful desire of the flesh is the same as killing it, because it is the same as if the desire were no longer there. A member of a Christian's body may scream its desire, but by God's grace a Christian will not listen. It is as if his member were dead.

The word "mortify" is a stern, decisive and uncompromising word. It implies that dealing with sin God's way means to be ruthless. Christians must cut off **any** opportunity to think of sin and avoid any situation that would feed their appetites for sin. That means they must limit what they see, hear and do. They must always be ready to separate themselves from any person or deny themselves anything that might encourage them to sin. They must take firm and deliberate steps to mortify the members of their sinful flesh. Do they hear dirty stories or gossip? They must walk away. Does the TV or radio program use bad language or present scenes and situations to which Christians should not expose themselves? They must turn it off. Does their eye wander to a place or a person that it shouldn't? They must look away, or avoid the person or place. As long as they live in their bodies on the earth, that is their full-time job.

As we mentioned in our examination of verse 2, sin is attractive to a believer's flesh, which has not yet been changed. A believer is aware that it is easy to develop an affection for sin. Yet a believer does not want to continue in his sin. He hates it like God hates it. He wants to deal with it how God will deal with it on Judgment Day (Col. 3:6). He is alarmed that sin has captured him for the moment, and he takes steps to "mortify" or kill it (Col. 3:5). By killing it, we mean that a true believer will take the necessary steps to turn away from anything that attracts him to sin. He will act to remove sin's influence in his life, so it is as if the sin does not exist for him, as if he has killed it.

We also must remember that sin is not an alien force that has invaded Christians' minds and bodies from outer space. They are not victims of an evil foreign agent who has taken them captive. In fact, they initiate sin. It starts with them, in their members. They are willing participants in sin because in their flesh they enjoy sin. It is a delicious habit to which their flesh is addicted. So, they are not surprised by sin unawares. In fact, the tendency of their members is to look for opportunities to sin. In their flesh, they too easily study to do their own will in opposition to doing what God says in His Word. So the call to "mortify" is urgent and insistent.

The word that best describes the intent of verse 5 is "repentance." At this point it is important to set aside some common misunderstandings about repentance. Repentance is not a word that means Christians regret or feel sorry about the horrible consequences of their sins, which they and others must bear, although that certainly is a proper Christian attitude. When he does sin, a true believer reacts in brokenness and sorrow. Neither is repentance a word that means Christians seek to do something to compensate for their foolish disobedience. Instead, repentance means to make a U-turn in the road of life and go the opposite direction, with purposeful strides away from self-desires and toward God's will.

In addition to that, the deliberate action which is the mark of repentance is not a virtue that makes Christians particularly endearing. They do not gain honor for turning away from something that they had no business doing in the first place. Recognizing the foolishness of doing something sinful and belatedly turning from it is an expected and obligatory action. Repentance may be a refreshing change from a former life of wickedness, but it does not change the facts. Repentance does not erase the record of the numerous and odious sins Christians commit, nor does it absolve Christians of those sins. Repentance may begin the healing process, but doing the right thing does not make someone a hero. Repentance is simply a necessary step in God's economy for dealing with sin. Repentance begins with Christians' eye-opening honesty about their own wickedness and continues with their deliberate steps away from it. A believer is candid about his situation and has a heart that earnestly seeks to turn from his sin and to please God.

It is hard to repent. Why? Sometimes we are afraid that we will miss some special joy. Sometimes "friends" encourage us to sin and we do not want to lose their esteem and companionship. But if we refuse to turn from our sin, we must wrestle with the fear and doubt that we may not be saved.

Despite the value of the wisdom that comes from verse 5, we must emphasize that repentance alone is not enough. A Christian may cease to do that which is wrong, but that restraint is not sufficient to gain victory over his sin. The complete picture is to replace the business of sin with the business of obedience. To the negative call to "mortify," verses 10 and 12 add the positive call to "put on," or in the words of Romans 6:13, "yield yourselves unto God." Christians are counseled to be busy, to use their time in holy pursuits (I Tim. 6:11). They must make an effort to fill their minds with anything that redirects their focus away from whatever tantalizes them to sin. They must seek to be occupied with service to God.

Verse 5 also uses the word "your." As we mentioned earlier, in any attempt to gain victory over sin, the spotlight must not be upon the sins of others, as obnoxious and numerous as they are. Nor should we dwell upon and crusade against the social injustices or the general moral depravity of mankind. That is just a ruse to take the blame off of our own sin. Besides, the sins of society or of mankind as a whole are nothing more than the collective sins of each person in that society, including "your" sin. As it turns out, Christians have no time to look upon any other person's sins because they should be too busy dealing with their own sins by means of prayer and Bible study (I Tim. 4:16). The emphasis must always be upon "your" individual personal sin. That keeps the effort to gain victory over sin simpler and more in focus.

We should also mention that the sins listed in verse 5 are all the same in the sense that they are all equally wicked. The word "idolatry" refers not just to "covetousness," but to all the sins in verse 5. Any sin is idolatry because it puts that desire above the will of God. Capitulating is to serve that desire rather than God. Therefore, the need to "mortify" is not related to how bad the sin is. Mortifying is always an important and urgent item on our agenda for gaining victory over sin, because there are no little sins (James 2:10).

Related to the idea of sin as idolatry is the danger of incomplete or selective repentance. Perhaps we can understand this danger by means of the following example. Imagine that a person becomes aware of his sins, one at a time, over several years. Also imagine that, as the person becomes aware of each sin, he modifies his behavior to conform more closely to what he reads in the Bible. Then imagine eventually the person is called to repent of a particular sin which he repeatedly refuses to forsake. At that point he should ask the questions, "Why am I apparently willing to repent of so many sins, but unwilling to repent of this particular one? Is it because it means too much to me? Is it my idol, which I must serve at all costs? Is it possible that my former pattern of repentance was not real, but just something I did in my own strength just to please other people or impress God?" The danger is that a person could look back upon his previous pattern of "repentance" and think that all is well with his soul, when in fact his Christian experience was really just outward and self-motivated. He also could think that his stubbornness in one particular sin is not so important, inasmuch as he believes he has turned away from so many other sins in the past. In other words, a person could turn from many sins and yet face one that seems impossible to abandon. Whether he eventually repents of it or not reveals the true devotion of his heart, whether to God or to the idol of his sin.

It is true that dealing with sin is a life-long occupation. On a Christian's last day on earth, there will be many sins in his life of which he should have repented but did not, either because he never became aware of them or because he died before he could deal with them as he should. And it is true that a Christian takes time to repent of some sins, resisting for a while any change in a sinful behavior which his flesh cherishes. However, when God brings a particular sin to a Christian's attention and calls him to repent of it, under normal circumstances he eventually will repent of it. The reason is that God is the source of true repentance (Acts 5:31,11:18, II Tim. 2:25). He creates in His people the desire to call upon Him for all things (Isaiah 57:19), including the desire and power to repent from sin. And He then answers their request (Psalm 37:3,4).

Colossians 3:6, "For which things' sake the wrath of God cometh on the children of disobedience:"

The words in verse 6 provide motivation for repentance. They remind us of the threat of an existence under condemnation and, by contrast, the relief of a future life without it (John 5:24, Rom. 8:1). In other words, as an encouragement to repent, verse 6 reminds us of "the wrath of God" upon sinners.

A great deal is at stake as people struggle with sin. Christ, the supreme authority, will appear. What will those people do who despise His authority and who show it by their abandonment to their carnal desires? If people's sins cause them to wonder about their spiritual situation, great! They must deal with it now before it is too late. In contrast to that, if their sins are not accompanied with a fear of wrath, horrors! For people who are headed for a Christ-less eternity in Hell have no fear of God (Psalm 36:1, Rom 3:18).

But true believers, who are not personally threatened by condemnation, who are secure in God's love, still find motivation to repent in the reminder of "the wrath of God." They understand the enormity of their sin, of the insult it is to God. They understand that God reacts personally in wrath against sin because it is meant personally, for sin is deliberate rebellion against God. God's wrath is a measure of how bad sin is and true believers are distressed that their sinful behavior is such a disregard of Him who has shown so much love to them and whom they claim to love. It is not that they feel sorry for Him or that He needs protection and cannot take care of Himself, but that they love Him and are ashamed for the personal offense against Him that their sin is. They are grateful that they have been given a heart to hate sin, an attitude that accompanies their salvation. Their awareness of the nature of sin is wisdom that motivates them to put legs on their desire to repent (Job 28:28).

The words "the wrath of God" also provides a practical tip in dealing with sin. It reminds us of God's attitude toward sin, an attitude which Christians must share. Sometimes we are afraid that if we give up our sin we will miss something special, some kind of irreplaceable joy. It is so easy to feel sorry for ourselves, and say, "Poor me. I deserve a little indulgence." However, verse 6 puts things in proper perspective. We must look at our sin the way God looks at it, namely, with hatred, as the word "wrath" implies. We must despise and loathe it for what it really is (Jer. 36:31). If we do not have that holy hatred for sin, then our battle against sin must begin there. We must ask God in prayer for the eyes to see how disgusting and repulsive our sin is to Him and ask for the hatred that He has toward it. It is easy, too easy, to be angry at the sin of others. But only God can show us the nature of our own sin and create in us an emotion that matches His.

In support of the need and value of hatred for sin, we read in Ephesians 4:26, "be ye angry, and sin not: let not the sun go down upon your wrath." This verse is not an accommodation to people's natural propensity to lose their temper. The verse is not saying, "I know that you are going to get angry. But at least don't get so angry that you lose control and sin. Make sure that you resolve your anger before the day is through." After all, anger is sin, as we read in Ephesians 4:31. That is, all anger is sin except one kind, the kind which Ephesians 4:26 points out. What kind of anger is that? According to Ephesians 4:26, it is the anger that leads us to "sin not." We recognize that as the anger against our own sin, the same anger mentioned in Colossians 3:6.

Incidentally, hatred toward our sin does not mean that we focus upon it and brood over it. That tactic leads to more sin and is really a form of pride. No, we must have a cool deliberate hatred that translates into a swift and decisive action. Then we can move on to "seek those things which are above," in order to do God's will in our lives.

Our hatred for sin is related to shame. Believers represent the Holy God in this world and are saddened when their sin dishonors Him. Our hatred for sin also is related to fear. Believers tremble at God's Word (Isaiah 66:2), knowing with great relief the disaster they escaped and knowing the terror of that awaits all the unsaved.

Colossians 3:7-9, "In the which ye also walked some time, when ye lived in them. But now ye also put off all these; anger, wrath, malice, blasphemy, filthy communication out of your mouth. Lie not one to another, seeing that ye have put off the old man with his deeds;"

The words, "in the which ye also walked some time, when ye lived in them," found in verse 7, provide some additional motivation for repentance. They remind a Christian of his horrid past life of enslavement to sin (Rom. 6:21). And, by contrast, the words highlight the joy of obedience that marks a Christian's present life of salvation (Rom. 6:17). Altogether, verses 7 through 9 remind us of the difference that can be expected between those who do not live under God's authority (Titus 3:2) and those who do (Titus 3:8).

Verses 7 through 9 are both humbling and encouraging. They are humbling in that they remind us of our shameful heritage (Titus 3:3). We always have a previous record that should check our tendency to boast in our present victories over sins and motivate us to be sympathetic and patient with other people who also struggle with sin. But the verses also are encouraging in that they speak of things gone by that no longer dominate us. We are never totally free of any of these things until we leave this earth, but they are no longer our master, a fact that is food for praise to an amazingly gracious God.

Next, let us turn to Colossians 3:10-17. These verses develop the second principle. They show how the power of the resurrected life within Christians shapes their affection so that they **do not want to** sin.

Colossians 3:10-14, "And have put on the new man, which is renewed in knowledge after the image of him that created him: Where there is neither Greek nor Jew, circumcision nor uncircumcision, Barbarian, Scythian, bond nor free: but Christ is all, and in all. Put on therefore, as the elect of God, holy and beloved, bowels of mercies, kindness, humbleness of mind, meekness, longsuffering; Forbearing one another, and forgiving one another, if any man have a quarrel against any: even as Christ forgave you, so also do ye. And above all these things put on charity, which is the bond of perfectness."

According to verse 10, Christians are expected to put on a "new man." One way to think about this is to recognize that the "new man" is Jesus Himself. It is Jesus within them (Col. 1:27). That is, Christians display a life that is "the image" of Jesus (Rom. 8:29), so what He wants is what they want. That is why they do not want to sin but want to do God's will.

Another way to think about this is to recall that a Christian is a new creation (II Cor. 5:17), created in Christ Jesus (Eph. 2:10). As a "new man," a Christian has a new "want to." Being a new man does not mean being a different person. God uses the word "new" in the Bible to mean fulfilled, especially in connection with the Gospel. The Old Testament is the Gospel promised. The New Testament is the Gospel fulfilled. Both testaments describe the same Gospel. It is just that the New Testament explains something new about it, namely, that it is completed in Jesus. Similarly, a Christian is new in the sense that Jesus dwells within him so that he can fulfill the purpose for which he was originally created. A Christian is free to serve God as his new, implanted life desires (Gal. 5:1,13).

According to verse 11, the expectation that a Christian wants to do God's will is independent of his background or life situation. All true believers are "raised in Christ" and want the same thing. What they now want as a "new man," or as an "image of him that created (them)" is described in verses 12 through 14.

Colossians 3:15, "And let the peace of God rule in your hearts, to the which also ye are called in one body; and be ye thankful."

The command "let the peace of God rule in your hearts" can be obeyed only by the people for whom Jesus is the supreme authority. Since Jesus, the Peace of God (Eph. 2:14), is the authority of all believers, they will not seek another. Jesus is the "peace" who rules over a Christian's heart and its affections by virtue of His redemption. In a way we could entitle Colossians 3, or the whole book of Colossians for that matter, as The Peace-Ruled Heart.

According to Luke 6:45 and 12:34, the kind of heart a person has is revealed by who rules over it. And that rulership is displayed through the life that he leads. That is, we can tell our own heart (I Cor. 11:28, II Cor. 13:5). We cannot necessarily tell another person's heart (James 4:12). After all, would we include David, who committed fornication with Bathsheba and was responsible for her husband's death, among the heroes of faith (Heb. 11:32)? If we did not have God's personal statement that he was a "man after God's own heart" (I Sam. 13:14, Acts 13:22) or if we did not read that his heart was smitten when the prophet Nathan accused him (II Sam. 12:13, Psalm 51:1-4), our verdict would probably be that David was unsaved.

But whenever sin comes into a person's own life, either because he listens to the rival authority of his own desires or the words of another person, he must always ask, "What is the matter with my heart that I don't love and serve God? Who is ruling in my heart?" As we mentioned before, the fact that sin bothers a believer is a good sign. It is a sign that sin is alien to his new nature; and he will once again, with God's power and wisdom, be set on the right way to walk.

The words in Colossians 3:15, "and be ye thankful," that is, "thankful to God," remind us of the importance of prayer in the business of dealing with sin (Psalm 32:5,6). The moment a believer begins to think about sin he should pray, especially prayers of thanksgiving.

The prayer of thankfulness means that a believer recognizes he is dependent upon God's care and has found God's supply in every needful occasion (Phil. 4:6-7,19). A believer recognizes that, in his struggle to turn from sin, he must walk one step at a time. Sometimes, as he seeks to stop thinking of the attraction of a particular sin, he must earnestly pray for God's help to take him through the next hour, or even the next minute. Then, as he finds that God has given him the victory for that span of time, he continues to pray for strength during the next hour or minute. Each succeeding victory gives him confidence to continue through the present struggle and gratitude for God's faithfulness. His success in dealing with sin vindicates his trust in his Lord to lead him moment by moment safely through each challenge.

The prayer of thankfulness also means that a believer recognizes all that the Lord has done for his salvation to prepare him for the hazardous Christian walk. Cheer replaces self-pity, as he focuses upon the blessings of God. He discovers the wisdom of the counsel that his mind must not be sin-occupied but full of the words and love of his Savior. He also discovers that he must be looking, not for an excuse to fulfill his own desires, but for an opportunity to complete God's will for his life (Matt. 6:10, Col. 3:23).

The prayer of thankfulness maintains the genuine peace and joy that sin cannot provide and that the world can neither understand nor take away. Above all, a believer is relieved and thankful that God is the supreme authority in the universe and that He is the Lord of his life. Knowing what a mess he has made in the past and could make in the future, he is happy that now Jesus is in charge.

Colossians 3:16-17, "Let the word of Christ dwell in you richly in all wisdom; teaching and admonishing one another in psalms and hymns and spiritual songs, singing with grace in your hearts to the Lord. And whatsoever ye do in word or deed, do all in the name of the Lord Jesus, giving thanks to God and the Father by him."

These verses state two excellent strategies for dealing with sin. One strategy is found in the words, "let the word of Christ dwell in you richly." Again, where does sin begin? It begins in our minds. We always think about the sin we commit. It doesn't ambush us. The counsel is that as soon as the thought of sin pops into our mind, we must ask for God's mercy to focus on His Word. Like a pot full of sand, that has no room for anything else, a mind full of God's Word crowds out evil thoughts. The idea is we must meditate upon God's Word when sinful thoughts assault our minds (Psalm 37:31, 119:11, Prov. 7:1-3).

Bible study and memorization are what a Christian does as part of his preparation in advance, before going out into the world and struggling with a particular sin (Rom. 13:14). It is not wise or possible to strap on a sword and armor when in the middle of a battle. Therefore, by means of prior Bible study and memorization, a Christian acquires abiding attitudes which can check his impulsive reaction to follow the appeal of his flesh, a reaction that may be hard to control in the press of a temptation. Also, through the Bible a Christian gains the insight and skill to make correct decisions in a complex and messy struggle with sin.

Another strategy is found in the words, "teaching and admonishing one another in psalms and hymns and spiritual songs, singing with grace in your hearts to the Lord." Christian songs are wonderful devices to train our minds to think about holy things, especially in the passionate, stressful and confusing times of temptation. The idea is that as soon as sinful thoughts enter our minds, we should replace them by "singing with grace in your hearts to the Lord" (Psalm 51:14).

However, according to verse 16, the music must both teach and admonish. And in I Corinthians 14:15, we learn that we must sing with "understanding," that is, with an understanding of the Bible. In other words, to be most helpful, the lyrics must be faithful to the Bible and be more substantive than simple repetitive choruses. The songs not only must be uplifting, as music often is, but also must include the darker reality of the consequences of sin, namely warnings about judgment (Psalm 101:1).

Our songs must be sung "to the Lord." That means, we sing songs that He would want to hear, rather than songs that are popular with the world and that satisfy our own carnal tastes. That is why our songs should be shaped by the Bible, for His own words are sweetest to His ears. The words "to the Lord" also mean that what we sing is a prayer. If we have "risen with Christ," the desire of our hearts should be, "Oh, may we not join the world that sings its wild and foolish melodies. May we join the host of heaven that sings praises of and to the Lord, the Creator and Savior of the universe!" (Rev. 5:9-10)

Colossians 3:18-22, "Wives, submit yourselves unto your own husbands, as it is fit in the Lord. Husbands, love your wives, and

be not bitter against them. Children, obey your parents in all things: for this is well pleasing unto the Lord. Fathers, provoke not your children to anger, lest they be discouraged. Servants, obey in all things your masters according to the flesh; not with eyeservice, as menpleasers; but in singleness of heart, fearing God:"

These verses illustrate the two principles. The passage shows how believers behave in different life situations, which reveals they can and want to do God's will. The everyday events of life will show that they have been "risen with Christ" and are under His authority. We can see the power of the resurrected life in believers' relationships to their marriage partners, to their children, and to those in the hierarchy of human authority above and below them. A Christian's own flesh affords numerous occasions to sin. To that we can add the many human relationships that either provide opportunities to sin or to demonstrate resurrection power. Let us briefly consider the examples these verses present.

First, let us think about the counsel of verse 18. Husbands can be foolish and abusive. They often do not deserve the submission of their wives. That fact could encourage the tendency of wives, as all people, to heed their fleshly desire to feel sorry for themselves and lead them to take more control of their lives. Yet the counsel of the Bible is that a wife "submit" to her husband. A Christian wife's submission to her husband reflects her submission to the Lord, and is a witness that she really is "in the Lord."

Next, let us think about verse 19. Wives are sinners, too. It is as easy to find a reason to be "bitter against them." That fact could encourage the tendency of husbands, as all people, to heed their fleshly desire to selfishness and impatience, and lead them to abrogate their responsibility to sacrificially care for their wives, as well as seek the sympathetic companionship of other women. Yet the Bible commands husbands to "love" their wives, not just in word but in deed. A Christian husband's love for his wife reflects the love that has been given to him in the Gospel.

Now, let us turn to verse 20. Parents can be hypocritical and unfair. They may be right in some things, but not in "all things." That fact could encourage the tendency of children, as all people, to heed their fleshly desire to rebel and lead them to both question and challenge authority. Yet the counsel of the Bible is that a child "obey." Christian children's obedience is not just to their parents, but also is a reflection of the fact that they are under the control of Jesus Himself and should seek to please their Lord.

From verse 21, we gain the following wisdom. Children can be immature, exasperating and unthankful. They often operate in a thoughtless and self-centered manner. That fact could encourage the tendency of parents, as all people, to react in kind, and lead them to set a poor example, which would encourage their children to sin even more. Yet the counsel of the Bible is that a parent "provoke not ... to anger." The word "anger" is not in the original Greek text and should be left out. The Greek word translated "provoke not," is used only here and in II Corinthians 9:2. It means "do not create a zeal by example." Parents must not set an example that will encourage their children in their natural zeal to sin. They must not react to their children in a way that would discourage them from following Jesus. Christian parents who are careful about their own walk with God before their children, show that they have been "raised with Christ."

Finally, we are given the example in verse 22. Masters can be unreasonable and tyrannical. They often can forget that their servants also are people, created in God's image, and order them about in an insensitive and even abusive manner. That fact could encourage the tendency of servants, as all people, to lazy indifference to duty or service that is motivated only by self-preservation. Yet the counsel of the Bible is that a servant "obey ..... in singleness of heart." Christian servants' obedience to their masters is not superficial but from the heart, and shows that they "fear God," who is their real Master.

Colossians 3:23-25, "And whatsoever ye do, do it heartily, as to the Lord, and not unto men; Knowing that of the Lord ye shall receive the reward of the inheritance: for ye serve the Lord Christ. But he that doeth wrong shall receive for the wrong which he hath done: and there is no respect of persons."

These verses describe the proper motivation that must be behind the application of the two principles.

Verse 24 teaches that Christians do not seek victory over their sin because they hope for some personal gain. There are no extra inducements, honors, or rewards dispensed to Christians in Heaven for anything they do on earth. Christians receive eternal life, the gift common to all believers, that is bestowed according to unmerited grace. The "reward" mentioned in this verse actually refers to God Himself, as we read in Genesis 15:1. That is, Christians do not just receive the blessings of salvation; they receive Jesus Himself (Col. 2:6). We must also notice that the reward is an "inheritance." That is, it is something bestowed upon them independently of anything that they have done in the past or do now. It is a blessing of sovereign grace.

Verse 25 teaches that Christians do not obey their Lord because they fear retribution or embarrassing exposure for their failings in dealing with sin in their lives. There are no reviews on Judgment Day for anything Christians did not do properly on earth. After all, the purpose of standing before the Judgment throne is always to pronounce innocence or guilt (Rom. 2:5-11, Rev. 20:12,13). Since all men are guilty sinners in themselves, anyone who must stand for judgment will be condemned and will experience God's wrath. Therefore the word "he," found twice in this verse, refers to unbelievers, for whom dealing with sin now is unimportant and unsuccessful. The relief for Christians is that Jesus has already withstood that judgment for all of His people (Rom. 8:3, Gal. 3:13, I Pet. 2:24). Their efforts in dealing with sin are their offerings of gratitude to God as part of sacrificing their bodies to Him, which is their reasonable service (Rom. 12:1,2).

Therefore, as verse 23 states, whatever Christians do, particularly to remove sin from their lives, they do "heartily." That is, the only true and acceptable motivation for serving the Lord is out of a right heart. Christians do not serve because they think they will be graded for their effort and then either gain or lose some blessing based upon their performance. Instead, they serve out of the love they have for their wonderful God and Savior (Col. 3:14,23), whose sacrifice is completely sufficient for all that they need. As we read in Romans 13:10, "love is the fulfilling of the law." Anything less is sin.

Chapter 4: What is Temptation?

The purpose of this chapter is to present a concrete and specific explanation of temptation. This is important because temptation is a companion to the idea of sin. Our understanding of and success in dealing with sin requires that we understand and successfully deal with temptation as well.

The word "temptation" is so familiar to people that they often assume they know what it means, even though they might struggle to give a definition or explanation of it. However, the word "temptation," has been greatly misunderstood, even by people who claim to be or who even may be believers. A sloppy and vague understanding of temptation, as in all other things, leads to errors of doctrine and eventually practice. The blessing is that the Bible provides a precise understanding of temptation. That understanding equips us to correctly answer some important questions about God's salvation plan. And that understanding guides us, as we struggle with sin and attempt to live a life that results in praise to God.

1. The Bible's idea of temptation

Sometimes we use the word "temptation" to refer to some object. We say, "that piece of pie is a great temptation." But the Bible does not use the word that way. Or we sometimes use the word "temptation" as a synonym for the word "attraction." We say "I hope I can resist that temptation." But the Bible does not use the phrase, "we resist temptation." These are confusing ways to think of temptation, that is, confusing if we are trying to understand what the Bible means by temptation.

James 1:2-3 tells us that temptation is a "trying" of our faith. James 1:12 repeats the notion that temptation is an event in which we are "tried." The word that we find translated "temptation" means a test, or an examination. I Timothy 6:9 tells us that temptations are what people fall "into." Also, II Peter 2:9 teaches that God delivers the godly "out of" temptations. Taking all this information together, we can say that temptation refers, not to an object or its allure, but to a test into which a person enters, even though the object may play a role in the test.

We can get a picture of the Bible's idea of temptation if we think of a schoolroom in which a student sits in a chair with a math test in front of him. Is he prepared to pass the test? A student and the test paper, together, make up a situation "into" which he enters. That situation, in time, will reveal if he is able to solve math problems or not. We call that situation an examination. That situation of a student and a test paper together is an accurate picture of the idea behind the word "temptation."

Another illustration of the Bible's idea of temptation is a mineral assay. For example, the old California '49ers brought their rock samples to someone who knew enough chemistry to test them for their gold content. Did their rocks contain gold? The chemicals applied to the samples showed if the yellow pieces were gold or iron pyrite, fool's gold. The assay or analysis was a test "into" which the samples were put, in order to reveal their true composition. Or, if you will, the assay was a "temptation."

Still one more illustration of the Bible's idea of temptation is magnetism. We must simplify the idea of magnetism for the sake of this comparison, but we can still make a few correct observations that will help us. A magnet always has a magnetic field in the space around it that causes an attractive force on iron, cobalt, nickel or similar metal. We may wonder if an object in our hand contains any of these kinds of elements. But all doubt will be removed if it is attracted to or not attracted to magnet. The piece of metal in the presence of a magnet is a test. Both parts together are needed to make the test. In a technical sense, for the sake of clarifying the message of the Bible, we can call this situation a "temptation." This magnetic illustration gives a more complete picture of the word "temptation" because it includes the idea that there is an attraction between the magnet and the metal.

These three illustrations help us correctly understand what the Bible says about the temptations we face every day of our lives. However, at this time we should say something that will help simplify our analysis. This is important because it will help us to avoid confusion and help us be accurate and clear in what we think about temptations.

People are attracted to many things. Some things to which people are attracted are good. God has created them that way. It is part of God's design for people to desire some things. For example, people are attracted to food when they are hungry. Similarly, clothes, shelter and companionship attract people, all for legitimate reasons. The Bible acknowledges that kind of attraction indirectly. However, those sorts of attractions are not the primary focus of the Bible's discussion about temptation.

People also are attracted to bad things. People are attracted to revenge, gossip, lust and many other things that are wicked. They are attracted to these things because they are fallen creatures, with bodies of flesh that are full of sinful tendencies. People also are attracted to good things but try to fulfill their hunger in a sinful way or at a wrong time. The attraction to do bad things or to fulfill the desire for good things in a bad way is part of the Bible's message of temptation because the Bible is concerned about the problem of sin. This is the attraction that is the focus of our discussion.

Incidentally, we can distinguish a bad attraction from a good one if we compare the situation with what the Bible says. Our consciences are only a limited guide. They first must be trained by the Bible to be reliable.

Remember, a temptation has two parts. One is a person and the other is something that attracts the person in some way. Both together comprise a situation that is called a temptation. The temptation is not the thing that attracts him. A temptation is not the attraction the thing has for a person. According to the Bible, a temptation is just a situation that is contrived, or deliberately set-up, to reveal the true nature of something. It is a test, an examination, an assay. It is as if a temptation were a drama in which there is an actor on a stage with one prop. The story line is that the actor is placed in the presence of a prop that he is told to reject. What he then does, in a certain way, reveals what kind of person he is. That is how the test works. Will the person embrace the object or will he ignore it? In time, he will reveal his heart's desire. He will either pass or fail the test. He will either pass or fail the temptation, depending upon what kind of person he is. As the Bible explains, the temptation is nothing more than a test.

At this point, it is important to clarify an important concept about temptation, in order to avoid a common but dangerous misunderstanding. As we have emphasized, a temptation is a test in the sense that it is a revealer. A temptation can be compared to a magnifying glass which is used to get a good look at what is there, but which in no way alters or improves what is examined. That is, a temptation is only a revealer and nothing more. A temptation cannot be compared to a ladder by which people ascend through their own efforts to a higher level of wisdom, strength or virtue. It is not as if a temptation is presented to people as an occasion for them to exercise their innate abilities so that they may gain victory over it and thereby acquire a strength of character they did not have before. People are what they are, and their response to a temptation is like an open window into their soul, revealing its true nature. For example, an unsaved person eventually will fail to obey in the face of a temptation and so reveal both his evil nature and his impotence to control its desires. However, a saved person eventually will triumphantly obey His Lord in the face of a temptation and so reveal his new nature wrought of God, who gives him the holy desire and spiritual strength that he displays in his victory.

This brings us to another important observation about how God uses temptations in Christians' lives. Christians' successful completion of a temptation is followed by ..... another temptation! So, after they pass a test, they can expect another test, sometimes a harder test, or a continuation of the same test. For example, Abram received the promise of a son when he was 75 years old (Gen. 12:1-4), a promise that was repeated more than once (Gen. 13:16, 15:4, 17:6-8). His test was that he had to wait for the fulfillment of the promise until he was 100 years old (Gen. 21:1-5). His test continued for 25 years. As we see, tests are part of Christians' life-long experiences. There are many reasons for this. The most important one is that temptations "worketh" virtues in the lives of God's people (James 1:3-4), and the grace that they demonstrate, as a consequence of passing the tests God sends their way, He wants all to see (Matt. 5:16). After Christians successfully face more and more demanding tests, the light within them shines brighter. That is, Jesus works in His people to do His will (Phil. 2:13). He is the light that men see as His people successfully deal with temptations (John 8:12). Therefore, in order that Jesus receive the glory, He brings his people into temptation to show what He has done and continues to do in their lives, as they reveal a dependence and trust in Him, in the midst of a difficult test (Job 23:10).

2. Some questions about temptation

Now we are prepared to answer some questions about temptation. We will not answer all possible questions, but we will look at some important ones.

One question comes to us when we wonder about the temptation of Jesus found in Matthew 4. Matthew says that Jesus was tempted of the devil. It also says that Jesus was hungry. Did Jesus sin? No, He did not. First of all, we must remember that a temptation is a morally neutral situation. It is neither good nor bad. It is simply a set-up used as a test, an examination, an assay, for the purpose of revealing the nature of what is tested. A person may fail a test. But the test itself is not sin. Instead, sin comes from the person who fails the test. So temptation is not sin.

Secondly, the Bible explicitly states in Hebrews 4:15 that Jesus was tempted but without sin. Jesus' temptation was not sin and neither are our temptations sin. It is true that Jesus had an appetite after 40 days without food. We have appetites, too. But the stones that Jesus could have turned into bread were not sin and the hunger Jesus had for bread was not sin. A temptation can be a situation that encourages our appetite, but the appetite is not necessarily a sin. We hunger for many different things. We can think of a temptation as an offer to fill that hunger. It is a sin to fill that hunger in a way that is against God's will. The issue is, what will we do in the face of a temptation? Will we be obedient to God or not?

Another question is "Does God tempt us?" Yes, God does tempt us. The Bible states that ultimately all temptations come to us from God. In fact, every test in life is from the hand of God, either directly or as He allows others to execute it. The support for this claim can be found in many places of the Bible. A few of them are Exodus 20:20, Psalm 11:4, Proverbs 17:3, Ecclesiastes 1:13, 3:10, Jeremiah 17:10 and Hebrews 4:12-13.

The answer to the question above helps us answer another question. "Does Satan tempt us?" The answer is yes (Matt. 4:3, I Thess. 3:5). He and all unbelievers do, but only as God allows them to set up a test. We must keep in mind that Satan is only a tool in God's hand. Always, God is in control of the nature and extent of the test (Job 1:12, 2:6). Christians are never tested beyond the ability of God to keep them secure in His love. Therefore, every object and event we encounter is a test, no matter whom God uses to administer it. All of life is a test, that is, a temptation.

At this point we must clarify God's and Satan's role in temptation. The words "with evil" in James 1:13 are the key. To properly understand this verse we can read it as, "Let no man say when he is tempted (with evil), I am tempted (to do evil) of God; for God cannot be tempted **with evil**, neither tempteth he any man (with evil)." God does tempt us, but it is not with the purpose to cause us to fall into evil sin. We cannot blame God for our fall into sin. The attraction for something evil comes from within us (James 1:14-15). If we are not restrained, we will fall. But that is not God's fault. On the other hand, it is always Satan's goal to cause people to sin. God may allow Satan and unsaved people to tempt us. Satan and unsaved people may desire our fall. But God is simply giving us a test to reveal what is in our hearts.

If we are prone to fall and many times do, is it wrong for God to tempt us? No. Again, temptation is just a test. It is not as if God is trying to discover what is in our hearts. He knows all men (John 2:24,25). The tests are meant to reveal or confirm our true spiritual condition to ourselves (II Cor. 13:5) and sometimes to others (Matt. 5:16, I Peter 2:12). If a test confirms that we are saved, then we will not continue with unfounded apprehensions about our salvation. If, through a test, we discover that we are not saved, then by God's grace we will not continue to live in the fantasy that we are saved, but seek God's salvation instead.

If God tempts us, then why do we read in Matthew 6:13 that we should pray, "lead us not into temptation"? Also, why did Jesus say to His disciples in Matthew 26:41, "pray that ye enter not into temptation"? The answer is found in the context of Matthew 26. Jesus is being weighed in the balance. He was in the middle of the greatest test of all, the test before God's Judgment Throne. Laden with the sins of His people, He was found guilty and condemned (Matt. 26:38,39). Therefore, in Matthew 26:41, Jesus is saying, "pray that you don't face the Judgment of God alone, as I now must. Pray that you will be saved from the trial that all unsaved people must face on their own at the end of time." That is the message of Matthew 6:13 as well.

3. Two reactions to temptation.

Having discussed the meaning of temptation and having answered a few questions about temptation, now let us consider how people deal with temptations, in failure and in success. In other words, we shall try to understand how unbelievers deal with temptations, and we shall try to understand the role temptations play in the lives of true believers. Actually we will be trying to answer the question, "Why do people fall or not fall into temptation?" and the related question, "How can they successfully deal with temptation?"

First of all, we must restate a principle. The principle is this: **every object and every event in life is part of a temptation for everybody**. The principle is another way of saying that every object and every event in life is part of a test for us. Life is really one big test. And this planet is one big testing arena. We have already shown from the Bible that this is so.

For example, the fact that we are born with certain abilities or lack of abilities is a test. Do we boast? Do we really give thanks for what we have? Are we impatient with others who do not have similar abilities? Do we murmur and complain that we do not have certain abilities? Are we resentful and jealous of others who have abilities we lack? In another example, the fact that we are born into a family order is a test. Are we an older child with younger brothers or sisters? Are we irritated that we are called to be responsible and an example to others or annoyed that our privacy is invaded by younger ones? Are we a younger child with older brothers and sisters? Do we complain that we do not get the same privileges our older siblings get? The fact that we are an only child is a test too. Are we self-centered, selfish and spoiled? There are many examples. Our work, our school and our recreation - all are tests.

From the point of view that a temptation is a test, the principle that we are tempted by everything may be acceptable to most people. If we think about it for a moment, we react in one way or another to everything around us. For example, some evil things attract us into doing something sinful, other evil things we ignore. But in one way or another, we react to the things around us. And how we react tells something about ourselves. It tells what we like and dislike. It tells what kind of a heart we have and whether we have the desire and power to refrain from indulging in things we ought to avoid. With all of this in mind, people can agree that every object and event tests us.

On the other hand, from the point of view that all the objects around us attract us to do evil, this principle is not acceptable to most people. In fact, it is offensive. After all, we are quick to point out that some things may be a problem for us, but other sinful things do not attract us at all. A typical reaction would be, "How dare you claim that I would lie, or cheat, or steal, or ..." It is true that some sinful actions are not a problem for us to the extent that they may be for someone else. But we are all sinners; and we all share the tendency to do every kind of sinful thing that is possible. The object or event that is part of the test reveals that tendency. Our personalities may be different from someone else's and may cause us to sin more or less easily in one area than another. But everyone without exception has a bodily desire for pride, for revenge, for gossip, for lust and so forth. It may be, at the moment in our lives when we are tested, we are not as easily attracted to one particular sort of evil, but our sinful human nature is attracted to all sins, any of which we would commit under the right circumstances. For example, a mother or a father who walks the streets of a bombed-out city during a war in search of bread for their starving daughter may lie, steal and kill to keep their little girl alive. If we argue against the fact that we are capable of any kind of evil, then we have a quarrel with verses such as Jeremiah 17:9 and Romans 3:12.

Let us remember that a temptation is a test that requires two things:

a person and an object or action which attracts the person to do evil. The question is, "What will a person do in the presence of something that attracts him to do evil?" If we recall our illustration of a magnet, a piece of iron will always jump to the magnet, unless it is restrained. Similarly, a person will jump to the object that he sees unless he is restrained in some way. The test then becomes a way to answer the question, "Is there some restraint in that person's life?"

What we mean by restraint is an **inner** restraint. God restrains all sinners to some degree, otherwise society would completely collapse (Gen. 20:6, 31:7, Rom. 13:3,4, II Thess. 2:6-7). He arranges restraints that are based upon outer circumstances. However, in our discussion of temptation, we mean the inner restraint of a saved heart.

Let us examine the two possible reactions to a temptation. Let us begin by asking a variety of questions. If we look at fifty people neatly dressed and quietly standing at a bus stop, they all seem nice. There seems to be no difference among them. But what happens when they are put to the test? What happens if they are handed a tract and thus face a gospel test, that is, a test to see if they trust God and want to do things His way? Or consider the situation of two people, one who gives in to his desires as he faces a temptation and another who does not give in to his own desires in the face of the same temptation. Why does one person fail and another person pass? Furthermore, if it is true that the temptation itself is not a sin because it is just a test, then at what point does his sin enter into the picture?

People sin in their minds, even when they are not in the presence of an object that might stimulate that sin. For example, since people are sinful, they think about revenge, even when the person they hate is not around. They think about something juicy about which to gossip, even when there is no one else around with whom to talk. In other words, people set themselves up to sin, they are self-prepared to fail the test and sin. The test just reveals that. So a temptation is a situation composed of two parts. One is a person who is prepared to sin. Another is an object that functions as a catalyst to evoke his sinful desire and action. The temptation is just a test to reveal what is already in the heart of a person.

The Bible is full of examples of failure in the face of temptation. Consider King Saul. He was told to wait seven days for the prophet Samuel before fighting the Philistines. Samuel did not show up at the appointed time, so Saul made an unauthorized sacrifice to God in preparation for the battle (I Sam. 13:5-13). Samuel's delay was the test. In the face of that test, Saul failed. But he was ready to fail because he had already failed the bigger test, namely, in his heart he did not trust God but trusted himself instead. His pride and self-focus led him to do what came naturally, to make excuses, justifications, alibis and rationalizations in the face of Samuel's accusations. Saul was right in his own eyes, no matter what. Without a restraint, King Saul sinned.

Now let us trace the steps a believer takes in the face of temptation. Let us consider Joseph's situation, of which we read in Genesis. All that Joseph did was based upon a deep trust in God, despite the abuse of his brothers and his subsequent enslavement in Egypt (Gen. 45:5,7; 50:20). When faced with the temptation to lie in bed with Potiphar's wife, Joseph knew that he should run from her rather than think about the physical pleasure and temporary advantage staying with her would give him (Gen. 39:9-12). Like Jesus in the wilderness, Joseph immediately rejected the object of attraction. Matthew 5 says we must be quick and ruthless with any situation that might cause us to sin, removing anything that would be a problem for us. As we read, it is better to go to Heaven with one eye than into Hell with two.

The question comes, "But don't people who claim to be believers fail tests?" Yes, many times. True believers are honest and can recall many of their failures. Believers fail for many different reasons. Sometimes believers try to analyze the temptation, but that only makes it so big in their minds they eventually feel they have to give in. Sometimes they forget their dependence upon God and foolishly think that they might be able to handle it correctly on their own. Sometimes, believers are surprised by a temptation and fail as a quick knee-jerk reaction. Sometimes they are not prepared because of their neglect of prayer and lack of time spent in the Bible.

However, a believer's failure produces an immediate response of godly sorrow. He agrees with God's word that accuses him. A believer does not focus only upon self and personal embarrassment. He focusses upon how his sin dishonored God's name. He also is smitten by the possibility that his sin may have hurt others in the sense that it contributed to their spiritual delinquency. That was the reaction David had when the prophet Nathan faced him with his sin with Bathsheba and Uriah (II Sam. 12:7-14). A believer's failure does not lead him to despair or surprise but reinforces a recognition that he is a sinner saved by grace and is in constant need of the care of his Savior. A believer's failure motivates him to be a more faithful witness from that point on (II Cor. 7:9-13). A believer's failure not only reminds him of the source of his strength, it also refreshes his love for his Savior who is always ready to forgive His children. That is, **having been saved**, a believer continues to live by faith in the promises of the Gospel.

We also must recognize that though believers do fail tests, they pass many times. In fact, as time goes by, they pass tests more and more frequently, even though they will continue to fail until the end of their lives on earth. That was the experience of Peter. He who once denied Jesus when challenged by a harmless servant girl (Mark 14:66-72), later spoke boldly about Jesus in the face of hostile persecution (Acts 4:8-13, 19-20). That is the confidence and joy Christians receive as benefits of passing a test. Their confidence and joy are based on the fact they see the value of being schooled by God through their tests. Their confidence and joy are based upon the fact they see the reality of God's power to help them pass those tests.

This brings us to another important truth that must be stated before we continue. Successfully obeying God in the face of a temptation is not equal to salvation. Salvation is not equal to a plan we can entitle "how to achieve victory over sin and temptation in two easy steps." In other words, if we want to properly understand the difference in the reactions to temptation between an unbeliever and a believer, we must understand the total picture. The foundation of understanding a person's reaction to temptation is a proper understanding of salvation.

In the first place, obedience or disobedience in the short term does not tell the whole story of a person's heart. The difference is in the long term. The difference between an unbeliever's and a believer's reaction to temptation is based upon the prior work of God's grace in a person's heart, something that is not necessarily evident immediately, but is revealed over time.

In the second place, only believers obey in the face of a temptation for the right reason. Remember, a temptation is only a test to see what is there. A temptation does not create something that is not there already. Therefore, salvation is not equal to victory over sin. Instead, victory over sin is an expectation whenever a believer is tested because it reveals God's prior work of salvation in his heart (Rom. 2:29, Heb. 10:16,22), even though his life history on earth will be sprinkled with failures. The questions we must always ask amid temptation or when evaluating our performance in a past temptation are, "Do I reveal God's work in me? Am I saved?"

4. Understanding Genesis 3:1-6: the anatomy of temptation

This passage provides a clear and important example of temptation. The lessons it contains are especially important for us as we seek to answer the question, “How do I successfully deal with temptation?” Let us examine some of the details.

Genesis 3:1, “Now the serpent was more subtil than any beast of the field which the LORD God had made. And he said unto the woman, Yea, hath God said, Ye shall not eat of every tree of the garden?”

While it is easy to focus upon the serpent as an agent of evil, as the Bible seems to do, we must keep in mind that the talking serpent was a beast that God had made as part of His “very good” created universe. Also, the Hebrew word translated “subtil” is a word for “prudent” (or wise), as we read in Proverbs 22:3. There is no animal to which we can compare it today, but it is enough to recognize that Eve was not surprised by its ability to speak and in fact carefully listened to it. There was no reason for her to fear it or be suspicious. It is not that the serpent was an evil creature itself. It was that Satan used the serpent for his dark and evil spiritual purpose.

However, Satan is not mentioned, either here or in the New Testament’s account of this story (II Cor. 11:3, I Tim. 2:14). Why? The answer can be found in a similar contest found in the book of Job. At the end of the book, God discusses with Job many things but never once mentions Satan’s wager and challenge that led to Job’s suffering. Again we ask, “Why?” Besides the fact that God does not owe Job an explanation for anything that He does (Job 33:13), God does not talk about Satan because Satan’s challenge was not the real reason Job suffered. God had things in mind that He wanted to accomplish in Job’s life and He simply used Satan as a supporting actor in the fulfilment of His purposes, one of which was that Job would know and trust God in a far deeper way than he had before he suffered. Job had heard of God, but now He had a first-hand experience of who God really is (Job. 42:5).

Similarly, Satan is not mentioned in Genesis 3 because the temptation in the garden of Eden was really God’s doing, not Satan’s. God created the forbidden tree and He put both Adam and Eve in the same garden with it. In allowing Satan to encourage Eve to eat of the tree, God simply used Satan to move His Gospel drama along, a role that Satan was eager to play. God had set up the testing arena He wanted in order to accomplish more than one purpose. As we shall see, through the test given to Adam and Eve, God teaches much about human nature and about His amazing love.

Genesis 3:2,3, "And the woman said unto the serpent, We may eat of the fruit of the trees of the garden: But of the fruit of the tree which is in the midst of the garden, God hath said, Ye shall not eat of it, neither shall ye touch it, lest ye die."

Notice that according to the observation of Eve, the tree of the knowledge of good and evil, the tree which was such a problem for her and Adam, was located "in the midst of the garden." Why didn't God put it in a remote corner of the garden, maybe in a place that was hard to find? Does it seem fair to put it where they couldn't possibly miss it and where it dominated the landscape? For one thing, it didn't really matter where it was because eventually they would have faced the temptation. But more significantly, its location reminds us of the fact that the test was a deliberate set-up by God, designed to reveal something about the nature of mankind. The tree's prominence in the garden highlighted the fact that God was forcing the issue because the whole episode was designed and administered by God Himself to test the two people He had made.

How we understand Eve's words, "neither shall ye touch it," depends upon an assumption we make about Genesis 2:16-17. One assumption is that what we read in Genesis 2:16-17 is all that God said about the tree of the knowledge of good and evil. Therefore, because Eve's words, "neither shall ye touch it," in Genesis 3:3, do not appear in Genesis 2:16-17, it is commonly taught that Eve was adding to the God's Word. If Genesis 2:16-17 is all that God said about the matter, then that is a valid point of view. It agrees with other verses in the Bible (Deut. 4:2, Prov. 30:6, Rev. 22:18). And it reminds us of the value of being faithful to God's Word when dealing with temptation.

However, there is another possible way to look at Eve's words. It is based upon the assumption that what we read in Genesis 2:16-17 is not all that God said about the tree of the knowledge of good and evil.

We should notice that a short, unknown amount of time passed between the Creation of Adam and Eve and the temptation. During that time, Adam and Eve experienced the fellowship of God, whose custom was to walk in the Garden (Gen. 3:8). Conversation with God would have resulted in more words than that which is recorded in the few verses in Genesis. Remember that accounts of the same conversations in Matthew, Mark and Luke differ because none give the full dialogue between Jesus and His disciples. Similarly, we know that Paul is not adding to God's word when he said in Acts 20:35, "I have shewed you all things, how that so labouring ye ought to support the weak, and to remember the words of the Lord Jesus, how he said, It is more blessed to give than to receive," even though we cannot read the words, "It is more blessed to give than to receive," anywhere in the four Gospels. With this in mind we could say that Eve's words in Genesis 3:3 were additional words God gave at another time.

Support for this view of Eve's words is based upon the fact that to add to God's Word is a sin. It is lying, saying something about God's Word that is not true. The Bible states in Genesis 3:11-13 that God condemned her for eating the fruit, as recorded in Genesis 3:6. God did not condemn her for adding to His Word, as recorded in Genesis 3:3. God never said, "You lied," even though Eve's words were spoken before she ate, and would have been her first transgression. According to the data found in the Bible, Eve did not disobey God until verse 6. That is the basis for the conclusion that the words, "neither shall ye touch it," are not a sinful addition but further instruction from God.

It is true that an outward act of sin is usually preceded by sinful thoughts and intentions. That is why some people look at Eve's words as evidence that she was already sinning in her mind. But that does not seem to apply in this case. The Bible does not say that she sinned before she ate the fruit. As we shall discuss below, we cannot pinpoint the exact second sin began. However, if we base our conclusions upon what we read in the Bible, we cannot claim that Eve must have sinned when she said, "neither shall ye touch it." From the information we have, both points of view are possible.

The value of the second view of understanding the words, "neither shall ye touch it," especially as we face temptation, is that it emphasizes we must not get near a situation that would lead us into sin. The counsel is we must flee sin. The wisdom of the words is obvious and repeated in other parts of the Bible. That was the tactic Joseph used (Gen. 39:12) and the counsel that Jesus gave (Matt. 5:28,29, cf. II Tim. 2:22). Clearly she was as well prepared as any human could have been when she faced the temptation.

Incidentally, the wise counsel to "get as far away from sin as you can" does not mean that we can totally escape the influence of sin. We would have to leave the universe to do that (I Cor. 5:9,10). A monastic life is no solution because the people who hide away in monasteries carry the propensity to sin within themselves. Nor can we pound a sign into the lawn in front of our house that says "Neighborhood watch. Sin-free zone," because the hand that holds the hammer is part of a body full of corruption. Besides that, we do not need to physically remove ourselves from all influences that would attract us to sin. With the Bible as our guide, we can recognize the dangers along our pilgrimage and avoid any unnecessary and obviously sinful entanglements. We find that we don't have to jump into a garbage can to know that it stinks. The perils soon become clear and, by means of God's power, avoidable.

Genesis 3:4,5, "And the serpent said unto the woman, Ye shall not surely die: For God doth know that in the day ye eat thereof, then your eyes shall be opened, and ye shall be as gods, knowing good and evil."

The words, "ye shall not surely die," direct contradictions of God's words, were red flags that should have warned Eve she was heading into trouble. At that moment righteous Eve was being watched by Satan to slay her (Psalm 37:32) and tested by God to reveal something fundamental about her (Psalm 11:4).

A temptation is tailored to fit a person's apparently most vulnerable spot. For example, after Satan showed Jesus all the kingdoms of the world, Satan's offer to Jesus was, "All these things will I give thee, if thou wilt fall down and worship me" (Matt. 4:9). Jesus came to earth to be the King of all the nations, and it appeared that here was a way to achieve that goal without going through the agony of the Cross. The appeal in Eve's case was to be more like Him in whose image she was created. That is a proper goal of anyone who loves God. However, Eve was already "as God" in all things that were important (Gen. 1:26,27). It is true that there was much she did not know. She knew good but she did not know evil. But she did not need to know everything to obey God. She knew enough to submit to all God said and trust Him for all He did not.

The words "for God doth know" imply Satan's objective was to encourage Eve to think God was knowingly or deliberately depriving her of something she ought to have, that God was cheating her. Satan knew that discontentment, not valuing what God has provided but wanting something more or different instead, is the parent to failure in the face of a temptation. But the evil of Satan's words was far deeper than that. Satan was encouraging Eve to believe the lie, "God doesn't really care about you." And yet, Eve had good reason to thank God for all His wonderful works, that were a blessing to her in the past and that she enjoyed in the present. Eve was obligated to trust God for all that was to come, and His rules were an expression of the fact that He wanted the very best for her. She never should have doubted His loving care for her.

At this point in the drama, it was just Eve and Satan in the garden. That is, she was flying solo. But God was only a prayer away. Did perfect Eve, perfectly educated Eve, think that she had what it took to take on the temptation alone, or did she recognize her need for God's help? That is the real question in this story.

Genesis 3:6, "And when the woman saw that the tree was good for food, and that it was pleasant to the eyes, and a tree to be desired to make one wise, she took of the fruit thereof, and did eat, and gave also unto her husband with her; and he did eat."

How did she know, when she saw the tree, "that the tree was good for food"? Maybe she guessed. But in the picture of how a temptation works, it made sense to eat the fruit from a human point of view. There were lots of apparently good physical, human reasons to eat. For one thing, it was a familiar tree. Eve probably saw it everyday. In fact, there could have been many other trees just like it in the garden. We do not know. The only unique thing about the tree we know for sure is that it was forbidden. For another thing, the fruit of the tree clearly was a source of food because it was not physically poisoning. The idea is that if people rely upon themselves and not upon God, they can always find an excuse or logical reason to convince themselves it is smart to give in to the temptation. It makes human sense to do it, especially if the object has an appeal that makes them interested in trying it out.

The moment Eve focused upon the tree her thoughts were no longer upon God but on herself. It was as if she had said, "I have a better idea than what God says." Maybe it was good food, inasmuch as it was part of God's good creation. However, that was not a deciding factor. It was an irrelevant point, even a fact she must ignore. The fruit was a temptation, not a source of nourishment.

Then we read, "it was pleasant to the eyes." That is part of the deception. If something looks good, can it be bad? If somebody is charming or nice, especially nice to you, can they be bad? If the show on TV (movie, magazine, book) is fun and slick (well made), but has only a few bad things, can it be a sin to watch, (read)? Can sin be nice? Can it come from nice people? Yes! Actually these are bad questions, questions that we should not ask. A wrong question to ask when faced with something attractive is, "What is so bad about it?" Instead, the right questions to ask, the questions we should ask are, "What is good about it? Will it help me be more faithful, a better witness? Does it glorify God?"

We are faced with good things all the time in life. Food is good. Friendships are good. So how do we know when something is really bad, no matter what it appears to be or what others say about it? One thing is for sure. We must not trust our own ideas. We must trust the Bible no matter what else seems to makes sense. The statement, "O Lord, I know that the way of man is not in himself: it is not in man that walketh to direct his steps," found in Jeremiah 10:23 is not just a comment upon the foolishness of sinful men; it is a accurate assessment of the design of human nature, whether sinful or perfect. We must never go it alone in life, especially when faced with a possibility to fall into sin.

Next we read, "a tree to be desired to make one wise." Eve showed wisdom in verse 3. Also she was made in God's image and on that basis she had a lot of natural wisdom. She was as wise as God had made her, and He had made her "very good." She was as wise as God had planned her to be at that time. But she saw an opportunity to be wiser. Today sinners cry, "I need to figure things out for myself. God doesn't know as much about my personal situation as I do. He doesn't know this modern world in which I must survive or understand my weaknesses and my desires. He doesn't realize how hard it is to turn from the object of my affection." Sin creates doubts about God and His Word, the Bible, in an attempt to reduce the Bible's credibility and therefore its relevance and authority. Simultaneously, sin elevates human wisdom.

When "she took," Eve did what she knew she should not do. The result of her close proximity and eventual contact with the object that allured her was that God went out of her mind. When a person gets deep enough into the clutches of the thing that attracts him, he gives in to the demands of his desires. In Eve's case, she thought "I might as well eat it now." Sin is never a surprise. There is always a time of preparation. The closer a person gets to sin the bigger sin gets in his mind. Familiarity with a sin, little by little, reduces a person's resistance to it. How often has a person said, "I didn't mean for things to get this far. Things just got out of control so fast!" Humans are too weak to get close to what leads them into sin and to continue to resist it alone. It is not wisdom, rather it is foolishness and sinful pride to say, "I can handle it." There is no virtue in relying upon ourselves. It is a conceited delusion that we are wise and strong enough to deal with sin alone.

Finally, she "did eat." At last we come to the deliberate act. No one forced Eve to eat. Actually at this point it was too late. The sin began the moment she desired it for food. The act was only the bitter flower of the seed that was planted before.

Genesis 3:6 continues with the words,"and (Eve) gave also unto her husband (Adam) with her; and he did eat." A person who sins wants fellowship in order to gain credibility in his own eyes and the eyes of others. Companionship in sin supports a sinner's a sense of righteousness or justification. The rationale is, "if everybody is doing it, maybe it isn't so bad, or I won't be punished, or the punishment won't be so bad, or I'll be overlooked in the crowd."

Eve would have been victorious if she had cried out to God, if she had depended upon Him for the wisdom and strength to obey His Word (Rom. 8:37, I Cor 15:57, II Cor. 2:14). A perfect Eve needed God. That was the way she was designed and put together. Adam's sin highlights that conclusion. I Timothy 2:14 is a great indictment of Adam in contrast to Eve. He sinned when he "was not deceived." Adam was tempted with the example of Eve's failure before him. Adam's eyes were wide open, so to speak. As a perfect man facing his wife in great peril, he should have fulfilled his role as a loving self-sacrificing husband. He should have cried out to the Lord on her behalf and offered his life as a sacrifice for hers (John 15:13, Eph. 5:25). Adam's sacrifice would not have been sufficient, because the payment for sin is eternal death. But he should have tried to help. Instead he forsook his advantage and selfishly joined her. Again, God is allowing the events of this drama to come to its tragic conclusion to reveal the fact that man cannot live independently from Him.

We see what happens when men try to do it themselves. The results are failure, shame, fear and condemnation. We learn that no man, even a perfect man, is a source of help. The drama reveals the amazing fact that what the first Adam would not do, the second Adam did do, as advertised on the Cross.

5. The value of temptations

We learned that temptations come from God. But why does God cause us to face temptations? What value do they have? Is there any reason to rejoice that we are tempted?

The Bible explains in James 1:2-4 and I Peter 1:6-7 that a temptation is a test with a purpose. The purpose is to reveal the work of God within a believer's heart to the end that God would be praised. A test is hard, but the Bible says in James 1:12-14 that God never tests someone in order to cause him to sin. We can never blame God for our failure. Failure is a testimony to the fact we are sinners and have no power or desire within ourselves to resist. I Corinthians 10:13 states that God gives us help through the power of the Gospel, and James 1:5 teaches that God gives help through His wisdom, which comes from His Word.

It is not too much to say that temptations are wonderful gifts of God for believers. First of all, temptations reveal to believers their weaknesses. As time goes by, believers learn what their weaknesses are. They are often surprised by the weaknesses they did not realize they had. Secondly, temptations remind believers of the patience and kindness of God. He gently puts up with all their past foolishness, and guides them through their present struggles with their sins. God pictures Himself as a Father who is always willing to receive and help His wayward children. Thirdly, temptations train believers, preparing them to face all the sin problems that God brings to their attention in the future. God knows they can successfully battle only a few sins at a time. God also knows that with each victory His children are more ready to deal with the next sin. Therefore, in God's agenda for their lives, He sets up a temptation as a controlled situation in which He guides them towards victory over a particular sin. In that way, when eventually they are victorious over a particular sin, they will be ready to face the next sin God brings to their attention. By means of the temptation, they will have gained experience in how dangerous sins can be, and in how dependent upon God's faithfulness they are. God causes His people to realize the truth expressed in Romans 13:14, that believers must be prepared ahead of time to deal with their sins.

Maybe the best way to think of a temptation is as an **opportunity** given to us by God. On one hand, if we are unbelievers, a temptation is an opportunity to do our own will no matter what, thereby revealing our wicked hearts. On the other hand, if we are believers, a temptation is an opportunity to do God's will no matter what, thereby revealing His holy heart through our behavior (Heb. 8:10).

Chapter 5: "Is sin so bad?"

The purpose of this chapter is to remind us how serious our sin problem is. This reminder is presented to motivate us to promptly deal with the sin that so easily besets us. This reminder also is presented to encourage us in order that we do not grow weary in our struggle against sin and abandon the effort. The Bible never pats Christians on the back and says, "Are you tired of fighting against your sins all the time? That's OK. You're doing fine. You need a break for a while. Let up a little so that you'll have the energy to face the struggle another day." Instead, the Bible is constant and unrelenting in its insistence that we fight against sin no matter what, because sin is so bad.

Sin is bad, very, very bad. It is bad for at least three reasons. Sin is bad because it is offensive. It is an insult to God. Sin is bad because it is corrupting. It results in physical, mental and spiritual deterioration, as well as death. Sin is bad because it is dangerous. It leads to the ultimate consequence of God's eternal condemnation and wrath in Hell.

1. Sin is offensive

Hatred toward God

Psalm 51:4 states, "Against thee, thee only, have I sinned, and done this evil in thy sight: that thou mightest be justified when thou speakest, and be clear when thou judgest." While people's sins often harm and distress other people and are a source of trouble to themselves, the Bible states that their sins are really directed against God (Gen. 39:9, Isaiah 65:3, Matt. 25:45, Luke 15:18, John 15:18).

All acts of disobedience are against God in the sense that all the laws in the universe are His. God designed, created and personally sustains the universe according to His Word. He is the Supreme Authority in His universe and has both the right and privilege to make all the rules. It is true that people in positions of authority make many rules, some helpful and even needful, others arbitrary, illogical and evil. It is true that other people are punished for violating those man-made rules. But the rules people make are legitimate only to the extent that their rules conform to God's rules. It is more than just that people's rules are flawed and ephemeral while God's rules are perfect, authoritative and abiding. The fact is that God is the only real rule maker. Therefore, when people sin it is rebellion against what He says.

All acts of disobedience also are against God in the sense that they are meant personally. People simply do not like God. In fact, we read in Romans 1:30 sinners are "haters of God." Matthew 26:67 displays the frightening destination to which the sinful heart of men takes them. According to that verse, sin leads men to spit in God's face.

The personal hatred unsaved people have for God is based upon the fact that they have an unholy fear of Him. That is, they have a dread of His justice, for they recognize deep in their hearts that they are accountable to Him (Rom. 2:14-16). The personal hatred people have for God also is based upon the fact that they are jealous of the competition His authority represents in their lives. For them, God's laws are oppressive. They are unreasonable burdens and infringements upon their perceived rights. People resent God's interference in their lives and despise Him for hindering them from pursuing and achieving what they want to do, even if it hurts them to get their way.

It might seem to be an exaggeration to say that sinners hate God, inasmuch as many people who are not saved are very respectful of holy things. Not only that, it might be confusing to say that sinners hate God because all saved people continue to sin until the day they die. So, can we say that they hate God, too?

Unsaved people do hate God, just as the Bible declares (Psalm 22:6, Isaiah 49:7, Acts 4:26,27). It might be that unsaved people have not been put in a situation that would expose the hatred that they may not even realize resides in their hearts. It also might be that some unsaved people's disposition and training may make their pleasant manners last, even under great stress. But if they are not saved, they are haters of God.

On the other hand, saved people do not hate God. They can think, say and do things that are contrary to God's law; and for a moment the outward appearance of their behavior is identical to someone who hates God. But their behavior soon becomes a great distress to them. For that and many other reasons, true believers eventually repent and turn from their sins.

The audacious and arrogant disobedience of unsaved people, motivated by their personal hatred of God, is shocking and breathtaking. We do not gladly think about it. But the Bible insists that we understand the awful nature of sin. Therefore, we shall briefly examine a few of the ways people express their hatred.

First of all, we shall consider the fact that when people sin, they are making a statement of their contempt for God's character and ability. They say in their heart, "God's laws have no value because God is not competent to make or enforce the right rules. God has no integrity because He is not just, since His rules are not fair." Sin is far worse than a cosmic brush-off, which says "I don't care about His rules." It is saying, "God is interfering where He doesn't belong. God is wrong to tell me what to do. Nothing He says is worth listening to." Again, sin is taken personally by God because it is meant personally by sinners.

Next, we shall think about Romans 1:18 which states that people "hold" (or as the word really is, "hold down") the knowledge of God. The idea is that people suppress the truth about God. Any time or place the truth of God is revealed, they seek to hide or distort it, in part because they do not want to answer to Him, and in part because they simply do not like Him.

One example of that suppression is given in Romans 1:23 and 24, which declares that sinners seek to "change" or rather "exchange" the reality of the glory of God with something imaginary. Instead of honoring God in their hearts and praising Him with their mouths for all of the beauty of His purity and holiness as well as the majesty of His power and authority, sinners seek to reduce God in their minds and advertise Him to be limited and fallible. They picture God to be something that He is not, by deliberately confusing the perfect Creator with His corrupted Creation.

In addition to that, Romans 1:25 states sinners "changed the truth of God into a lie." It is not possible to change the truth of God into a lie. But it is possible to make a statement about the truth of God, either a verbal statement or a statement through actions, that is a lie. To act in a wicked way and claim that God agrees with and approves of it is to claim something about God that is not true. In other words, sin is an offensive lie motivated by a desire to discredit God and dismiss His authority.

Next, we shall consider the fact that the "invisible things of" God are clearly seen in His Creation (Rom. 1:19-20). That is, there is a picture of God in what He has made, the clearest image being in the children of Adam (Gen 1:26). Therefore, unsaved people work extra hard to try to deface that picture. They do it by means of their immodest and sometimes grotesque outward adornment. They do it by means of their vile behavior (Rom. 1:24-27). Unsaved people try to erase any similarity between themselves and God because they do not want any reminder of God or His demands upon them. Also, people focus their malice upon one another as an attack against someone who is made in God's image. Consciously or unconsciously, people who sin are trying to suppress the witness to God that is found within and around themselves.

Perhaps we can better appreciate this terrible idea by means of the following illustration. Imagine that you gave a picture of yourself to someone whom you liked and whom you thought liked you. What if that same person, in gleeful meanness, defaced it right in front of you? What if he wrote horrible insults over it, tore it up and then threw it in your face? What if the person laughed over your dismay? How would you feel about that contemptuous attitude and action? In a similar way, all sins are mean-spirited, hateful, personal insults against God. God takes sinful disobedience to His law personally because it is meant personally by those who disobey Him, whether the person who sins consciously realizes it or not.

We also can think of unsaved people's hatred of God in the following way. It is as if we can measure the evil nature of sin when we consider the nature and character of the Person against whom it is committed. Perhaps the following illustration will serve, in a dim way, to clarify this idea. In one sense, the act of deliberately damaging a cheap, common vase and the act of deliberately damaging an expensive, rare vase are the same. Both display the callous and violent attitude of the vandal. But in another sense, the two acts are very different. The difference is in the value of the vases. One act results in a greater loss than the other. In a similar way, sin's enormity is based upon the fact that it is deliberately disobeying not a common person but the greatest of all Persons (Isaiah 40:25,26, 1 Timothy 6:14-16).

With all this in mind we can begin to understand the ugly and offensive nature and character of sin. God is beautiful in holiness. God is majestic in power and authority. God is worthy of prompt and adoring obedience because of who He is. Denying Him what is due Him is great wickedness. Therefore, sin is ugly and disgusting because it is deliberate, willful rebellion against the pure, holy and "incorruptible" God.

The hatred of people toward God is especially saddening when we consider that God is so kind and deserves thankful respect and submission for His gracious and undeserved blessings (Rom. 2:4). But sinners bite the Hand that feeds them. Sinners greedily grab the blessings that God showers upon the just and the unjust (Matt. 5:45), but are unwilling to thank Him for what they receive (Rom. 1:21).

Love for self

A sinner's hateful attitude toward God is related to his proud attitude toward himself. We can see the connection between them in Jeremiah 2:13, where we read, "For my people have committed two evils; they have forsaken me the fountain of living waters, and hewed them out cisterns, broken cisterns, that can hold no water." Of the many sins that the nation of Israel committed, God reduced them to two. One is that they would not go to God for their needs. They did not trust God (Jer. 2:5; Rom. 14:23). A person who sins says, "God's way is not good, at least not for me." We have already discussed that attitude.

The other sin Jeremiah points out is that they worked hard to provide for their own needs, because they trusted in themselves instead of God (Psalm 12:4, Prov. 12:15, Jer. 1:16). It is not just that sinners say, "God's way is not good for me." They also say, "My way is better than God's way." A person who sins trusts that his own way will make him happier or solve his problems in a better way than will God's way. Therefore, sin is a label that describes a person's deliberate disobedience to God's law that is motivated by a confidence and trust in himself, in replacement of a trust in God.

People's self-trust is based upon self-love (II Tim. 3:2). They show, at least at the moment they sin, that they are totally self-absorbed, self-centered. They are charmed by their own selves, impressed by their own philosophies and achievements, and protective of their own interests. They have no concern for God or anyone else, except that they may use other people to serve their own desires. The reason is that they hold their own desires to be the highest good for themselves.

This helps us understand the phrase "I am a jealous God" (Exod. 20:5, 34:14, Deut. 4:24, 5:9, 6:14,15). The phrase does not mean God is supersensitive, or that He can't handle competition, or that He can dish it out but He can't take it. Rather it is a reminder that when people sin, they give to another the love they owe to God alone (II Tim. 3:4). He is the worthy One who alone deserves to be the object of people's love. In that sense, all sin is equal to spiritual adultery and fornication.

Taking one more step down into the cesspool of sin, we come to the horrible description of sin found in I Samuel 15:22,23. There we read, "And Samuel said, Hath the LORD as great delight in burnt offerings and sacrifices, as in obeying the voice of the LORD? Behold, to obey is better than sacrifice, and to hearken than the fat of rams. For rebellion is as the sin of witchcraft, and stubbornness is as iniquity and idolatry." What a shock! Disobedience is equal to witchcraft and idolatry. Sin's identity as idolatry is somewhat easy to understand.

When people sin, they show that they value and honor their own way above everything else and sacrifice all for that sacred cause. That is, people's sins are really self-worship, and their idols are themselves. For support of this idea we can turn to Colossians 3:5. Colossians 3:5 lists many vices and sums them all up as "idolatry." That is, the word "idolatry" refers to the whole verse and not just the last vice of "covetousness." The reason sin is equated to idolatry is that sinners are devoted to their own wicked desires and serve them as they would a god.

Sin's identity as "witchcraft" is harder to accept. Yet, it is just as valid. For according to John 8:44, Satan is the father of all unsaved people, who serve and obey his lusts. Satan is the sworn enemy of and is at war with God (Rev. 12). He is eager to recruit anyone to help him in his battles against God. People who live lives of sin are really Satan's servants, honoring his cause.

Love for God

Finally, we can understand the offensive nature of sin when we compare the attitude that motivates a person to sin to the attitude that motivates a person to obey. That is, we can further understand how bad sin is when we consider the character of obedience.

When Jesus gave the apostle Peter a new command, after his previous cowardly, sinful denial of Jesus, He didn't ask him, "Will you obey me?" Instead, He asked, "Do you love me?" (John 21:15-17). Peter's obedience would not be evaluated simply by observing his outward compliance. The reason is that while sin certainly includes any behavior that does not conform to God's commandments, it encompasses much more. Wickedness is actually a heart problem (Jeremiah. 17:9).

As we read in Romans 13:10, "love is the fulfilling of the law," with the greatest love being a love for God (Matt. 22:37-38). Obedience is rooted in a heart attitude of love for God, an attitude upon which hangs "all the law and the prophets" (Matt. 22:40). Obedience to the law of God is summed up in the obligation to love God, and therefore to love all that He says, with all our heart, soul, mind and strength (Deut. 6:5, Mark 12:30). Anything less than a 100% heart commitment to doing God's will is sin.

Therefore, people sin because they **love** to sin rather than **love** to obey God (Prov. 2:14, 10:23, Jer. 5:31). In the first place, they love to sin in the sense that they love to think, say and do those things that satisfy their own desires. The world holds a great attraction for them and appeals strongly to their flesh. When people sin, they demonstrate that they cherish their own desires and fondly indulge the yearnings of their own flesh. So, people are in love with themselves, and are constantly seeking to give themselves what they want. They reveal that adoration by their deliberate disobedience to God.

In the second place, people love to sin in the sense that they love to think, say and do those things that are forbidden by God simply because He forbids them. Sinners are the kind of people who want to be the captains of their own souls, and they seek to wrest control from God. In fact, people are not always attracted to the tempting object they desire nor are they always enthused about the rebellious action they do, although that is often the case. Rather they cherish their imagined independence and express that presumed freedom by thinking, saying and doing anything that is different than what God commands. If God commands it, their sinful heart compels them to want, to love, the opposite.

The relationship between sin and the heart helps us understand an important response to personal sin that must be evident in the life of anyone who claims to be a Christian. A theoretically perfect record of obedience to God's law without the motivation of love for Him is not really obedience to the law (I Tim. 1:5). And in fact, in light of Romans 13:10, it is sin. We used the word "theoretically" because no one can ever attain to a perfect record on his own. The reason is that obedience requires an attitude of love, and love is a gracious fruit of the Holy Spirit given only to believers (Gal. 5:22). According to Romans 8:9, we either have the Spirit (and are saved), and show that fact by our love for God, or we do not have the Spirit (and are not saved), and show that fact by our lack of love for God. A person who is not saved and does not have a heart that loves God does not have the power or desire to obey God. So a "perfect record" without love is only a theory to discuss and is not a real possibility. We used that hypothetical situation to highlight the necessary ingredient of love in the recipe of obedience that is acceptable to God.

Since love for Jesus is demonstrated by means of obedience (John 14:21-23), the questions we must ask when we disobey are, "Do I love the Lord Jesus? Why don't I love Jesus, that I have done such a thing? What kind of heart do I have that it demonstrates no love for God?" And since it is also true that obedience is a product of God's saving love for us, we also must ask, "Does my attitude and behavior reveal if I am loved of God? Am I saved?" (II Cor. 13:5)

2. Sin is corrupting

Credit and blame

The universe was created very good, without one blemish (Gen. 1:31). Then Adam disobeyed God, and sin entered into the perfect universe (Rom 5:12). God's just response to Adam's sinful disobedience was swift and severe. God cursed the universe and its inhabitants, the effect of which was deterioration and eventual death (Gen. 2:17, 3:17, Dan. 9:14, Rom. 8:20). Although God claims credit or responsibility for the damage to which the universe is subject, as well as the sadness and pain humans endure, mankind gets the blame. It is ultimately because of Adam's sin that the universe and all who live in it groan under the heavy hand of God.

The fact that people live in a world that is sin-damaged and deteriorating more every day, resulting in hardship and sorrow (Psalm 32:10, Proverbs 13:21, Romans 2:9), is an automatic consequence of the wicked acts of their race (e.g. Romans 1:27). From that point of view, even though sin is a label for people's deliberate disobedience, we also can think of sin in terms of the corruption that results from it.

It is important to investigate some of the present consequences of sin. In that way we will better appreciate sin for the enemy it is, both to our environment and to ourselves. Let us, then, consider some of the ways in which sin has corrupted the universe and all who inhabit it.

Sin is opportunistic

Hebrews 12:1 states, "let us lay aside every weight, and the sin which doth so easily beset us." The Greek word translated "weight" is used only in this verse. But it is related to the word translated "hook" or "anchor." The words "which doth so easily beset" are a translation of a word that means to lie around idly. The idea of the verse is that sin is opportunistic. It lies around waiting for the chance to catch someone (Gen. 4:7). We can compare this idea to a hook in water. It is as if sin goes fishing with bait on a sharp hook. The lure must be deceptive to be effective. We could compare the bait to sin's promise of happiness, fulfillment and life, and the deadly hook to sorrow, vanity and death (Rom 6:23, II Thess. 2:10, Heb. 3:13). Or we can compare this idea to a virus. It is as if sin were an infectious pathogen that waited around, biding its time. When given the chance, it entered into and sickened the universe and all it contains. And it continues to infect the lives of people today. Sin is an effective infecting agent because it is wrapped in a coat of lies, lies that people so willingly believe and ingest. The only antidote to the infection of sin is the Gospel of God.

Corruption of the physical environment

Let us consider passages like Jeremiah 4:23-27, Hosea 4:1-3 or Joel 1:9-13. There are many others like them in the Bible. One message of these verses, in addition to their Gospel dimension, is that the physical deterioration of the environment in which people live has a spiritual basis. It is not that a particular abuse of the physical environment necessarily can be linked to a particular sinful action, although the foolish deeds of people does contribute to the damage the environment endures. Rather, it is that the sinful rebellion of people against God has resulted in a universe that is subject to the burden of a relentless curse. The many observable evidences of corruption in the physical world that are the present effects of sin are severe, pervasive, indelible and inescapable. There is no hope for the world in its present state. In fact, it is God's plan to remove this universe and replace it with a new one in which dwells righteousness (Isa. 65:17, Rom. 8:19-23, II Peter 3:10-13).

Even though it is easy to see the effects of sin in our physical environment, we must not make the mistake of limiting our understanding of sin to its physical consequences. We are material people and naturally have a material view of all things, including our problems. However, sin is not a "thing," an object that can be isolated from its environment. Sin cannot be compared to an insect specimen that we put into a glass case. We cannot type a label that says "sin vector," attach it to the display, and put it on a table for all to see. Also, when we say sin is "in us," we do not mean that sin can be found behind our left third rib, or inside our spleen. Neither can we put a drop of our blood on a microscope slide and see molecules of sin floating between the blood cells. It is true that sin betrays its presence through many physical ways in our lives; but, as we have discussed, it is a word that describes a spiritual situation.

We should add that the programs which many people design and carry out in an attempt to protect their physical environment are sad wastes of their time and energy. A respect for the physical universe is proper as part of our respect for its Creator. After all, it is His universe, and we are only His guests. However, the plans of many people to clean up the environment are misplaced. The problem is not the garbage in people's back yards. Instead, it is the garbage is people's hearts. The great zeal that many people demonstrate to "save" the physical environment reveals that the physical universe is an idol which commands their religious affection, trust and loyalty. Their fervor reveals their alarm that their god is dying. But their efforts are doomed to failure because God Himself is guiding the corruption of the world now and its eventual destruction at the end of time. Only in the Gospel will people find the solution to the deterioration of the universe. That is, only when people find salvation for their souls in the Gospel will people understand that the present unrighteous universe is God's tool to accomplish His spiritual goals (Luke 16:9). Only after people are saved can they understand that the hope of living in a perfect environment is the hope of Heaven (Isaiah 65:17, Rev. 21:1-4,23).

Corruption of relationships

Now let us consider the testimony of a passage like James 4:1-5. Sin causes problems between people. We are especially sensitive to the interpersonal conflicts and estrangements which are a measure the sin-caused social deterioration. The brutality and uselessness of violence and war between people causes us great distress. In addition, sin complicates life. People cover lies by more lies to avoid discovery. Divorce leaves indelible life-long scars on all people involved and requires strange and unnatural living arrangements, especially when children are involved. Arguments distort relationships and destroy friendships. Civil battles lead to legal complications, high costs and bitter hearts.

Unsaved sinners are so totally self-absorbed and self-preoccupied with fulfilling their own desires, so willing to justify themselves and condemn others, so driven to protect their pride and dignity, that they become egotistical monsters. People are rude, discourteous, impatient, angry, hateful, jealous, fearful of personal loss, haughty, critical and aggressive. We could supply a long list of examples. Yet, all are just symptoms of a deeper problem. The basis for the outward person-to-person conflict is the inward person-to-God conflict in people's hearts and in their resultant personal corruption.

Personal corruption

In addition to person-to-person problems, is the individual physical, mental and spiritual deterioration that accompanies personal sin. First, let us think about physical corruption that is displayed in people's bodies. We are aware of the physical disfiguring effects of disease, and the debilitating effects of injury. They are partly consequences of the general corruption due to God's curse and partly consequences of people's foolishness. Notice the sad testimony found in Romans 1:24, "Wherefore God also gave them up to uncleanness through the lusts of their own hearts, to dishonor their own bodies between themselves." That is, sin is self-deforming.

Some of the physical effects of sin in a person's body are clearly evident and dramatic. They are repulsive even to unbelievers, such as the results of drug abuse and promiscuous sex. Some of the physical effects are more superficial and subtle, but just as hideous. For example, how often have pretty girls or handsome boys ruined their appearance by selfish and discourteous speech and behavior? People may spend lots of time and money to improve and maintain how they look, but there is nothing as ugly as sin. While the beauty of holiness sparkles no matter how physically unattractive a person may be, the scowl of anger, the pout of stubborn self-interest, the sneer of criticism and the leer of lust are grotesque and repulsive distortions that mar even the most physically appealing features. Sin is the worst graffiti there is because it spoils the image of God on earth found in human beings.

Secondly, let us think about mental corruption. According to Ecclesiastes 9:3, "the heart of the sons of men is full of evil, and madness is in their heart." A person's madness can be based upon a physiological disorder, which is a consequence of God's general curse upon the universe in response to sin. Madness can also be induced by a specific traumatic incident or a prolonged foolish pattern of behavior which leads people to lose contact with reality. But in all cases, madness is a testimony to the effects of sin. Let us consider some of the ways in which madness is expressed.

Unsaved people are mad in the sense that they are irrational and illogical. For example, they claim they are no more than an evolved animal and have no more value than a tree. They also claim God is either like themselves or a product of someone's imagination. And yet, they cannot live sanely in the world of their own making. People can pretend that the human emotion of love is no more than a chemical reaction, or that existence is trivial, without any purpose, without any God-ordained objective or hope, but they cannot live like that. They cannot look into the eyes of someone for whom they care and treat them as they would a rock. They cannot get up in the morning without any reason for living. And yet, tragically they insist upon speaking and acting, not out of what makes sense, but out of their own imaginations, regardless of how absurd and ridiculous it may be.

Unsaved sinners also are mad in the sense that they are erratic, bizarre and capricious. They lack any reasonable self-control. Their actions make them seem like marionettes dangling in the wind, driven with no more aim than the present breeze of whim and fancy. They behave according to their impulsive and fickle, sinful desires.

Finally, unsaved people are mad in the sense that their sins are insane challenges to God. They are willing to take on the Almighty Creator and Judge of the universe (Isaiah 45:9). That is a contest the outcome of which is not in doubt, namely their certain physical, spiritual and eternal deaths. Such audacious and self-destructive defiance of God is spiritual suicide. How could anyone continue such foolishness? He could, only if he had no fear of God. It is no wonder the Bible talks about the "mystery of iniquity" (II Thess. 2:7).

Thirdly, let us think about spiritual corruption. In Ephesians 2:1 we read that a person is dead in his sins, apart from the grace of God. We all live with the great handicaps of broken and corrupt bodies, as well as a hostile environment, all of which are the results of sin. But according to Ephesians 2:1, the worst present effect of sin is a dead soul. Although they are alive in their body, unsaved sinners are dead in their souls. That means they are totally depraved, or controlled by the desires of their sin-infected bodies without any restraint from their dead souls. One important lesson of Ephesians 2:1 is that unsaved people do not have a free will to choose to obey God (Rom. 8:7,8). They are not able to obey His call to salvation. They have a free will to make many secular choices, such as what to wear or what to eat. But unsaved sinners do not have the free will to love God or obey His will. They are "dead" in their trespasses and sins. Since the effect of sin is to make people spiritually dead, a condition in which unsaved people remain, unsaved people cannot do anything to make themselves right with God; neither do they want to do anything about their spiritual problems.

When we say that unsaved people are "totally" depraved, we do not mean that unsaved people are as bad as they could be. They could be far worse, for God restrains the sin in people's hearts. Otherwise they would destroy themselves and the world in which they live before God completed His plans for this earth. Nor does the word "totally" mean that people cannot choose or do any human good. People are capable of choosing and doing many acts of human kindness, yet all of their actions are as filth rags (Isaiah 64:6), inasmuch as they do them with their own honor and not God's honor at heart. The word "totally" means that the poisonous effects of sin have reached to all parts of people's lives (Genesis 6:5).

The word "totally" also means that unsaved people are "totally" without any ability or desire to do anything that pleases God. The phrase "the way of the transgressors is hard" found in Proverbs 15:13 does not mean sinners make life difficult for themselves. It does not mean that troubles come to sinners because of their sin, although such an idea is true. Instead, it means sinners are hard-hearted, obstinate, unwilling and unable to change. The reason is that all people are "totally" dead in sin (Eph. 2:1). Since they are spiritually dead, unsaved people cannot do any spiritual or saving good, even if they wanted to (Rom. 8:7,8), and no one wants to (Rom. 3:10-12).

The word "totally" means sin is enslaving (John 8:34, Rom. 6:16). Sin is the oppressing tyrant of unsaved sinners. Sin is an unbreakable habit that leads nowhere else except to more sin (Rom 1:21). Imagining themselves to be free, unsaved people are compelled to do the bidding of their flesh. Unsaved people are in bondage to a horrible monster. It is as if sin was a voracious beast, with an insatiable appetite, which they serve to exhaustion (Isaiah 44:12). Such is the bondage to which unsaved people are subject.

The fact that unsaved people are spiritually dead also leads to the conclusion that people are driven to disobey God's law because they **are** sinners. It is their nature to want to sin. In other words, people disobey for no other reason than they are the kind of creature that does not want to do God's will, whatever that may be. We must not accept the premise that men are "basically good," but occasionally do some bad things. Nor should we be surprised that "nice" people can sometimes act very wickedly. Rather, the evidence is that evil follows men wherever they go. The reason that sin is so handy and portable is that the desire to sin resides within everyone. Outside of the grace of God, all people's hearts are desperately wicked, and their sin is simply an expression of who they are.

3. Sin is dangerous

The most important and urgent problem of all

In Ezekiel 18:4 and Romans 6:23 we read, "Behold, all souls are mine; as the soul of the father, so also the soul of the son is mine: the soul that sinneth, it shall die ..." and "... for the wages of sin is death."

Sin is bad for sinners because it results in their death.

Physical death is a dramatic change. It ends all of the hopes for which we yearn and all the fears that haunt us. It puts aside all of our sweet achievements and bitter failures. Physical death breaks all of our earthly ties to family and friends. It separates us from all our earthly enemies and all the claims of society upon us. It cancels all of our burdensome and insistent earthly obligations. Physical death is a final and unalterable event. It is a universal experience and an inevitable appointment. Unless the world comes to an end before we die, physical death ends our personal earthly existence (Eccl. 3:20). For those reasons alone, physical death is the most important event we must face on earth.

However, physical death is important for a much greater reason than all those we have given. Physical death is not the end of our existence. Physical death is not equivalent to annihilation. Physical death is the end of our contact with physical reality, but it is not the end of all things. We have more than just a body; we also have an eternal soul that continues to exist beyond the grave. The physical death we see calls our attention to the more important spiritual problem we cannot see. We see physical death, and the Bible tells us the meaning of what we see.

The real importance of physical death is that it is a door that leads to a meeting with God (Heb. 9:27). God is on the other side of death's door and it is to Him whom we must give an account for all that we have thought, said and done. The results of that accounting is the most horrible and frightening event of all: abiding under the wrath of God without any hope of change, ever. That destiny is called eternal death. Therefore sin is dangerous, not only because it leads to physical death, but also because it leads to eternal death.

The most important issue of life is not preserving our physical life, nor regaining and maintaining our physical health, if we are sick. The most important issue of life is not achieving a respected and useful education, nor using that education to succeed in a career. The most important issue of life is not attaining financial security, nor acquiring the real estate and other material objects which such wealth affords. The most important issue of life is not grasping political power, nor using that power to try to make a better society and environment. The most important issue of life is not finding the meaning and purpose to our existence by means of self-understanding and self-fulfillment, nor by means of our identification with our family and friends. Instead, the most important issue of life is to avoid condemnation and Hell.

Much to the surprise of many people, the most important issue of life is not even sacrificially serving others nor faithfully serving God (I Cor. 13:1-3). As it turns out, even if a person had a noble desire to serve others or God, he cannot fulfill that desire without first dealing with the most important issue of all, his personal sin and the wrath that it merits. In fact, he really does not want to fulfill that desire, at least not in the way that God has commanded. Again, the most important issue of life is to be sure that we will not face the wrath of God in punishment for our sins after we die (John 3:36).

A person's meeting with God after physical death is not in itself a problem. If God asked a person for an accounting and was pleased with his response, that person would experience none of His wrath. But that is not how it will be. If Jesus is not a person's Savior and has not stood for judgment on his behalf, then his meeting with God leads to wrath. The reason is that, when he will give an account to God, a neutral event in itself, it will be revealed that none of his thoughts, words and deeds measured up to God's standards. A sinner's behavior is different than what God demands in His law. That difference leads to condemnation, followed by eternal death in Hell. So it is really the difference between God's expectations (as expressed in His Law) and a sinner's performance that is the basis for the great problem he faces after death. That difference is called sin. It is because of sin that an unsaved person is in such trouble with God. Sin is the source of all his problems, problems for which he must seek wisdom, especially wisdom to avoid God's wrath after he dies.

Thus, the Bible explains that physical death is a reminder that all unsaved people face the ultimate consequences of their sin, eternal death. Eternal death is real and is far more horrible than we can imagine. All people are forced to recognize the fact of physical death but most refuse to acknowledge the sin that causes it and the condemnation and spiritual death that follows it. Some people recognize the deeper problem of sin but focus upon its physical consequences, including physical death. Therefore, we must direct people's attention to the bigger and more tragic spiritual reality in order to find a way to avoid an angry God before it is too late. **Sin is the most important and urgent problem we face on earth.**

Sin is dangerous because it puts people in harm's way. It leads to death, physical and eternal death, exposing them to the condemnation and wrath of God. We have discussed all that at length. But more than that, sin is especially dangerous because it obstructs people from finding the only rescue available from the threat of God's wrath. First of all, sin encourages people to despise the truth and modify their view of the Gospel (Prov. 1:7, 24:21, I Cor 1:18, Col. 2:8, II Thess 2:10-11). It is as if every sin has a string attached to it that can be traced back to the cross. That is, a person's view of sin and the Gospel are related to each other. Sin causes people to soften or dismiss the Gospel's threat of judgment, because they wish to avoid the uncomfortable reminder of the threat of condemnation. Sin seals off their minds from a careful consideration of their spiritual need to avoid the wrath to come (Prov. 22:3). Secondly, sin is like a narcotic (Prov. 6:9, I Thess 5:6-7). Sin deceitfully causes people to continue indulging their desires. It causes them to fill their senses and minds with the satisfaction of their passions, unrestrained by their consciences and God's law. It is as if they are intoxicated or living in a dream, heedless of the spiritual jeopardy into which their sin places them.

Judgment as a measure of sin's nature

This brings us to the point of view that another way to measure the evil nature of sin is to consider the punishment God requires to pay for it. God is absolutely righteous (Psalm 11:7, 119:137, Rev. 16:5). He requires no more or less than what is fair to pay for disobedience to His law (Rom. 6:23). The punishment exactly fits the crime. From that point of view, we see that sin is so bad that it requires the payment of eternal death in Hell (Rev. 21:8). One great display of that fact is the sacrifice of Jesus. The shame and horror of the Cross is that it advertises how serious an offense sin is. Therefore, judgment is a measure of sin's evil nature.

Yet there is hope. The help that people need but often refuse is only a prayer away. When a person cries out for help and receives grace to recognize that he is a sinner and realizes that he must meet a pure and holy God, he is not left alone with the fear that grips his heart. He also has the good news of the Bible's message about sin. He has the wisdom of the Bible that begins with fear but ends in hope. Only someone who has been given the grace to fear, will seek a way to take that fear away. The Bible shows sinners that Jesus is the Way (John 14:6). From that we see that the Cross also advertises "God so loved the world, that he gave his only begotten Son, that whosoever believeth in him should not perish, but have everlasting life" (John 3:16).

Chapter 6: Some more questions about sin

The purpose of this chapter is to answer various questions about sin and temptation that we did not previously consider, or discuss sufficiently. We have collected them in this separate chapter so that the answers would not interfere with or confuse the discussion in the main part of this book.

1. "Why is sin part of the universe in the first place? If sin has resulted in such a mess, why did God allow Adam to sin?"

If we ask these questions out of our pain and sorrow as a complaint, or out of our anger as an accusation, or if we think that God is inept or unfair, then we will find no answers. One thing is for sure, the presence of sin in the world is not God's fault. Nor is it evidence of God's defective workmanship in Creation. God made everything very good. The ultimate reason God allowed Adam to sin is a mystery we cannot fully understand now. That limitation in our knowledge is humbling and reminds us of Who is in control of the universe (Deut. 29:29). The Bible states that we have a fundamental obligation to submit to all that God has revealed in His Word and trust Him for all He has not revealed. We must do that without full prior understanding, based solely upon a trust in God's character and competency.

Nevertheless, there are some good answers that explain a lot to those who submit to the authority of the Bible. The universe that God created, which includes space, time and the people who inhabit it, is an arena in which God tests what He has made (Prov. 17:3) in order to show something important about mankind and about Himself. Through Adam's sin, God is able to display many things.

For one thing, God displays something about the nature of man. Adam's disobedience revealed the fact that even a perfect, sinless man in a perfect uncorrupted environment can sin. Man cannot maintain his perfection by his own effort, without the help of God. When Adam was tempted to eat of the forbidden fruit, his response should have been to cry out to God for strength to remain faithful. The message of the Bible is that a perfect man is by nature totally dependent upon God to continue to remain perfect and sinless.

For another thing, God displays something about Himself. The depth of Adam's and all of his descendant's subsequent personal corruption reveals how much God had to do and was willing to do in order to free His people from the burden of their sin. That is, God was able to reveal His amazing love (Rom. 5:8). In addition to that, the depth of mankind's corruption reveals God's amazing competency, as He flawlessly executed His salvation plan despite the impediment and opposition of a sinful world (Acts 4:25-28).

2. "Why does God punish sinners?"

Even though sin is as terrible as we have previously described, it still is fair to ask, "Why does God punish sinners?" After all, if God insists that we forgive, why does He judge? Doesn't He tell us to love our enemies? Besides that, isn't He big enough to forgive and forget? Can't He let by-gones be by-gones?

Is it because people's sins are so odious and obnoxious that they deserve to be punished? Their sins certainly are disgusting. For that reason alone we should not be surprised that God reacts in wrath to those who hate Him and who show it by their deliberate disobedience. The terror and horror of God's wrath is equal to the wickedness of men's sin. Men are as wickedly ungodly and unrighteous as the wrath of God implies. Therefore, punishment will come to them for all of their sins, as we read in Matthew 12:36-37 and Revelation 20:13-14. However, the punishment of sinners is not first of all based upon how wicked their thoughts, words and deeds are. The Bible says there are no levels of sin. Every sin is equally bad (James 2:10), beyond limits so to speak, and ripe for judgment.

Ultimately, God punishes sin because He **has** to. First of all, God must punish people for their sins because He said He would (Gen. 2:16,17). He must keep His Word (Num. 23:19, Rom. 3:5,6), He is the God of Truth (Deut. 32:4, Psalm 31:5, John 14:6). He cannot lie (Num. 23:19, Rom. 3:4, Titus 1:2, Heb. 6:18).

Secondly, God must judge sinners because He is Sovereign, in total control of His universe (Isa. 40:21-23, Rev. 4:11). We can understand this reason in the following way. If people disobeyed God's laws with impunity, without any fear of consequences, and if people escaped the consequences of their sins, then they would do what is right in their own eyes and what satisfied their own personal desires. They would be in control. God's moral laws would not apply as He has stated. His laws wouldn't mean anything. Also, He would not be able to hold anyone accountable for their behavior. Therefore, He would not be God, the One who has total, absolute and final authority over all that He has made.

Thirdly, God must judge sinners because God created people in His own image. That means, among many other things, that God created people to be as righteous as He is (Matt. 5:48, I Peter 1:16). That is, God holds people to the same standard that He has for Himself. It is not that God is a slave to His own laws, but that God is who He is and His laws are statements of His character. He expects all people to display the same character He has, and holds them accountable for the difference. Anyone who is found guilty of sin, which reveals a character that is different than God's, will endure the wrath of God. The Cross showed that. That is, God would not spare His own Son but judged Him who bore the sins of His people. God's integrity was displayed in His judgment upon Jesus, which guaranteed the judgment of all who are condemned and must bear the punishment for their own sins.

****

Incidentally, our assurance that salvation is real is based upon the fact that judgment is real. Jeremiah 32:42 states, "For thus saith the LORD; Like as I have brought all this great evil (judgment) upon this people, so will I bring upon them all the good (salvation) that I have promised them." Judgment and blessing go together. In fact, judgement shows mercy is certain. What is the connection between judgment and salvation?

For one thing, God claims that He can do both (II Peter 2:9). If He cannot keep His Word to punish, then how do we know if He can keep His Word to save? Judgment Day for unsaved people has not yet occurred inasmuch as the end of the world has not come. Yet there is a taste of judgment upon the world now, in the form of God's curse, whose physical consequences even affects God's people. This preparation for judgment, and the actual event of Judgment Day, show that God means business in all that He says, both to punish and to save.

For another thing, God's judgment upon Jesus was the guarantee of salvation for His people. Not only did it provide the complete payment for sin that was required by the Law, but it also revealed God means what He says and that the fulfillment of the statement, "the wages of sin is death" (Rom 6:23) is a certainty. If His Word of condemnation will not be compromised, even to spare His own Son, neither will He modify nor cancel His promise to save His people (Rom. 8:32).

However, we must be careful when we connect judgment and

salvation. Judgment is an obligation that is based upon the integrity of God's Word, and therefore the honor of His character. Judgment is His automatic, inevitable response to sin. We said God punishes because He **has** to. In contrast to that, however, God's salvation is not automatic or inevitable. God saves people because in His own counsels He has decided to save some. Once He decided, He self-obligated Himself to be merciful to those people whom He had promised to save. So, we can say that God saves because He **wants** to, for His good pleasure and glory (Eph. 1:5-6, Rev. 4:11). In other words, punishment is a wage that must be paid but salvation is a gift that is pledged and bestowed by grace.

When we see the tokens of the final judgment such as the increasing evil in this world, we must not be fearful and unbelieving. We must flee to the Savior. The brokenness of this world shows that the Lord knows how to judge. Therefore, we are sure that He knows how to save. The present evidence that God is able to judge shows that His promised salvation is secure. When we see the token of the final judgment, we find comfort in the sure word of prophecy, for He who promised final judgement, promised complete salvation, too.

3. "Does God hate sinners?"

In Romans 1:18 we read, "the wrath of God is revealed from heaven against all ungodliness and unrighteousness of men." These words seem to support the common misconception of sin that is many times expressed as, "God hates the sin but not the sinner." Such a view implies that sin is an evil object or malevolent force independent of people, or that sin is some enemy from whose clutches poor people must be rescued. That kind of thinking is very widespread and terribly wrong, and Romans 1:18 does not really support it. Although Romans 1:18 does say that God's wrath is against unrighteousness and ungodliness, people are the ones who sin. Sin exists because people exist. Therefore, God does not punish sin. He punishes people. He does not send sin to Hell. He sends people to Hell.

Any attempt to separate people from the sin they commit is artificial and dangerous. It leads to the doctrinal perversion that God loves everyone in a redemptive way, when in fact not all people are redeemed. It also leads to an emaciated Gospel mandate that states Christians must not scare people into Heaven by talking about Hell and damnation but only show them God's love in word and in deed. However, the Bible states that God hates the workers of iniquity (Psalm

5:5, 11:5, 26:5, 31:6, 139:21,22, Amos 3:1, Zeph. 2:5). Therefore, it is the job of every believer to warn all men of the danger into which their sin places them (Ezek. 3:16-21, II Cor. 5:9-11). If salvation is anything it is a rescue of people. It is a rescue, not from the moral and psychological manifestation and consequences of sin, but from the hands of an angry God (Heb. 10:31), Who will see to it that sinners receive the punishment they deserve (II Thess. 1:8, Heb. 12:29).

Romans 5:10 supports this idea. It states, "For if, when we were enemies, we were reconciled to God by the death of his Son, much more, being reconciled, we shall be saved by his life." Also Colossians 1:21 states, "And you, that were sometime alienated and enemies in your mind by wicked works, yet now hath he reconciled." It is true that Satan is the sworn enemy of God and encourages people to sin. Satan also seeks to suppress God's truth as well as remove God's image from man. But we cannot blame Satan for people's personal sins. From Romans 5:10 and Colossians 1:21 we learn that sinners are enemies of God, and that includes all the hatred we expect between enemies. As we learned previously, people's sins against God are meant personally. Therefore, God punishes people personally in response.

And yet we might wonder, "Does God hate people before they are saved?" What we have said so far about God's attitude toward sinners certainly applies to all people who die unsaved. In the sense that those people whom God intends to save are truly His enemies before they are saved, we could say that God's attitude is the same as it is toward any of His enemies. However, in as much as those people whom God intends to save were always included in His Gospel plan, designed in His love before the foundation of the world, it is too much to say that God hated them before they were saved. That is, all of God's enemies are not the same in His eyes. In themselves, all sinners are the same. There is no difference (Rom. 2:11, 3:9). However, by sovereign grace, God decides to make a difference and elects some to be His dear beloved children (Rom. 5:8, 9:11-13).

Having said all of that, we must hasten to add that the Bible speaks much of God's love, including His love for sinners (I John 4:10). It is His love that drives Him to display His grace to people who do not deserve it (John 3:16). Only the Bible revels a loving God. And it is the call of those whom He loves in Jesus to carry that message of love to the world.

Nevertheless, many people will remain under the wrath of God for eternity, just as many people will experience His blessings of love and grace forever. But to whom these different destinies apply and why the end of each person's life is not the same are not given for us to know (Deut. 29:29). We can only say what the Bible does and submit to the words we read in Psalm 18:30, "As for God, his way is perfect." That applies to His expressions of wrath and love.

4. "Are some sins worse than other sins? Are there less serious 'venal' sins and more serious 'mortal' sins? Are there big sins and little sins? For example, are there "white" lies that are less punishable if they result in good? Are actions that are against the law of God condoned if they are done for a good reason?"

The answer to all of these questions is, "No." It is true that some sins leave more noticeable marks upon the lives of people than other sins. It is true that some sins are more readily infectious and habit forming than other sins. It is true that some sins lead to a separation from the means of grace. It is true that some sins are private, affecting only ourselves, while others are public, affecting other people. It is true that some sins have more and lasting consequences in this life than other sins. However, the amount of embarrassment or pain our sins cause ourselves and other people, as well as the amount of serious and lasting consequences that result from our sins, are not a measure of the anger of God against those sins.

According to James 2:10 and I John 5:17, all sins are the same. In support of this, we should notice that the Tenth Commandment is the same as the First Commandment because if we covet, we place the object of our desire before God (Exod. 20:1-17). The object becomes our idol.

Also, committing a sin in order to accomplish a good purpose is based upon the premise that the ends justify the means. But that notion is really a statement of unbelief. It is saying that we cannot always trust God to work things out according to His will, but instead must assist Him by working things differently, otherwise His purpose would not be accomplished.

Therefore, all sins are equally terrible, no matter what the apparent result may be and no matter what motivation we think is behind it. All sins are rebellion against God.

5. "Do unborn children or little babies sin? Are they accountable to God?"

The answer is, "Yes." All people are sinners from conception

(Psalm 51:5, 58:3). The size of a person's body or the level of his physical and mental maturity does not change his spiritual condition. A soul does not change its nature according to its age on earth. The statement in Proverbs 22:15, "Foolishness is bound in the heart of a child," applies to children of all ages. All people need salvation, even small children and babies. Wonderfully, some are saved even before they are physically born (Luke 1:41).

Jesus' visit to the temple at age twelve is not an example of a person leaving childhood and becoming of age. That is, little children are not innocent and then become threatened by the wrath of God and Hell when they reach an imagined "age of accountability." If that were so, then it would be better if all children die at a young age in order to guarantee for them a place in Heaven.

As a corollary to this, we should mention that, when we have the opportunity to bring the Gospel to a child, we must not have the idea that some biblical topics do not apply to children and so should be left out of our presentation. It is appropriate to use simple and clear sentences, having in mind their smaller vocabulary, rudimentary grasp of grammar and limited life experience. But all subjects to which the Gospel speaks must be included in what we say. That means we cannot avoid the ideas of sin and judgment. As it turns out, little children are able to understand more than we usually think. But more importantly, they need to hear the complete message of the Bible because, if they are not saved, they are yet under the threat of God's judgment.

6. "Could I commit a sin that is so bad that it will never be forgiven by God? Can I ever be beyond hope? What about the 'unforgivable sin'?"

When someone's heart is smitten with remorse for the sins he has committed, he must remember the principle of Isaiah 1:18. As long as someone is physically alive, there is hope. There is always a way back to God (John 14:6). A person need only seek God for grace and mercy (Isaiah 55:6-7), that He would grant him the inclination and power to humble himself before God. Also, a person need only ask God for the ability to trust in His promise of mercy, made possible by the sacrifice of Jesus Christ (Psalm 80:17-19).

If a person fears, it may be that he has a reason to fear. He may not be saved. But help is still available in the Gospel (II Cor. 6:2). If a person fears and is saved, it may be that he has been playing with a sin and is not ready to give it up. It could be that God is graciously working in his heart in preparation of pushing him to repent. Sin is behind all problems that a person may have. Therefore, it is always good for a person to review his fears, turn away from what is precious to his flesh, and turn toward what is important to God.

Having said all that, let us now try to understand the words, "hath never forgiveness," found in Mark 3:29. First, we should set aside some wrong ideas about what people call the "unforgivable sin." The unforgivable sin is not the same as committing a really bad sin, a sin so offensive to God that He is unwilling to forgive it. Otherwise no one would be saved, because the Bible states that all sins are the same (James 2:10). We must also reject the idea that the unforgivable sin is equal to refusing to believe in Jesus, or to resisting His Gospel call. All people do that before they are saved. Finally, committing "the unforgivable sin" is not the same as following another religion and calling the Gospel "not the way of salvation." Before people are saved, they all believe in something else, even if they believe only in themselves.

What, then, do the words, "hath never forgiveness," mean? What is this sin, also called, "blaspheme against the Holy Ghost"? Another verse that might help us is I John 5:16. Let us try to understand the phrases, "a sin which is not unto death," and "there is a sin unto death: I do not say that he shall pray for it." These are troublesome words to some people. The second phrase especially worries people. After all, how can a person possibly have any hope of salvation if he might have committed a sin for which he can never pray for forgiveness?

All sins are sins "unto death" in the sense that the consequence of sin is eternal condemnation in Hell (Rom. 6:23). Therefore, the idea of the phrase "**not** unto death" must refer to a sin which is not liable to that penalty. The idea is that if a man sinned and it was "not unto death," that is, it did not lead unto his death in Hell, it is because he found salvation in Jesus Christ. The reason that the sin is "not unto death" is that Jesus removed the condemnation and the subsequent penalty of eternal death under the wrath of God by taking the penalty upon Himself. Maybe, to be most accurate, we could say that the phrase means "not unto the death of a sinner who believes," for it was "unto Jesus' death," in as much as Jesus died for a believer's sins.

On the other hand, in contrast to what we just concluded, we could say that a sin "unto death" is the sin of a person who remains under the condemnation of God. I John 5:16 adds, "There is a sin unto death ... I do not say that he shall pray for it." Therefore, we are forced to understand the words, "there is a sin unto death" to mean there is a special sin for which there is no provision made on the cross because, according to I John 5:16, there is no use praying for the forgiveness of that sin. There is no use praying for a sin for which no payment has been made. The person who sinned that sin must face the judgment of God on his own without the benefit of a substitute.

The only sin recorded in the Bible which fits that description is the sin commonly called "the unforgivable sin," as we read in Mark 3:29. That sin is defined as accusing Jesus of operating with the power and the motivation of Satan (Mark 3:22,30). Jesus is the only Savior which the world has and ever will know (I John 2:2). If a man decides and is fully convinced in his heart that Jesus is really working for and with the devil, then he has no other savior to turn to for salvation from the wrath to come. This seems to be a very special sin, not commonly found among even the most wicked men. A person who is guilty of this sin would never want the salvation of the Lord, because he thinks the gospel is not the promise of salvation. He is not concerned whether the gospel of the Bible is true or part of his life.

Therefore, anyone who is concerned that he may have committed a sin that is beyond forgiveness, has not. The fact that a person worries about it is a good sign. That attitude of alarm reveals that he has a fear of God. Anyone who sincerely believes Jesus is of Satan is not worried about this sin, or his standing before God, at least not on God's terms. But, of a man who is worried that he might have committed the "unforgivable sin," one thing is for sure. He could not be guilty of the "sin unto death" mentioned in I John 5:16.

However, he should not find any solace in the fact that he is worried, if he stops there. That worry ought to drive him to deal with any sin that makes him feel distant from God. He ought to seek reconciliation with God and put his worries aside. In fact, the Bible's statement of the sin against the Holy Spirit is a test for all people. The question is, will that concern lead a person to self-examination, cause him to appeal for mercy, and result in his trusting God's word of forgiveness? Or will the claim that he has gone beyond the point of no return be used by a person as a prideful excuse for refusing to submit to God's Gospel plan? Will he, in perverted self-righteousness disguised as despair, continue on a path of his own choosing?

Incidentally, we do not know a person's heart. We must leave the decision of a person's destiny up to God alone. We must never decide that someone has committed a sin "unto death" and cease praying for them. Everyone we meet is a candidate for prayerful evangelism.

7. “What will happen to me if I die at the time that I commit a sin? For example, what if I commit suicide, or die because of my foolish carelessness? Will I be forgiven if I die before I can ask for forgiveness?”

First of all, salvation is totally a work of God, independent of anything that a person does. God alone places all of a person’s past, present and future sins upon the Redeemer. God alone works in a person’s heart to give him a new life. After someone becomes saved, no one can do anything to change that permanent standing before God.

Therefore, salvation is not dependent upon the action of asking for forgiveness for each and every sin, nor is it rescinded if someone neglected to ask for forgiveness for a particular sin. If God has paid for a person’s sins because He intends to make that person His child, then God will incline that person to ask for forgiveness for any sin that He brings to his attention, in faith and with a contrite heart. But a person’s request for forgiveness has no spiritual value or power in itself. His prayer for forgiveness is only evidence of the fact God has already paid for all his sins and is already working in his heart. The power of salvation rests totally in the Gospel (Rom. 1:16). The Gospel is a once-for-all work of God, that even a sin committed at death cannot undo (Rom. 8:1, John 5:24).

Secondly, everybody has many sins for which they have not prayed at the moment they die. No one would ever be saved if salvation depended upon asking for forgiveness for each sin, especially since we commit many sins of which we are unaware. Remember, salvation is a work of God that is dependent upon nothing, at least nothing we do or do not do. If we are saved, our actions cannot change our standing before God.

A sin such as suicide is dramatic and without recourse. It is understandable that people consider it to be particularly evil, especially when we realize that it is self-murder. No wonder people ask, “Can someone who commits suicide be saved?” As we stated, “Yes, he can be saved because salvation is totally a work of God, independent of his performance.”

However, if someone is in such deep despair that it leads him to take the extreme action of suicide, he displays a lack of trust in God. It is the same as turning his back upon God, as if God were no one to rely on for help. Anyone can sin like that momentarily and do something that will not allow him to think things out more rationally later. But the fuller answer is that we leave the spiritual destiny of other people in the hands of God. It could be that the person only appeared to be a believer, until his lack of trust in God was revealed under duress. It could be that the person was a believer who lacked a faithful habit of prayer and Bible study. At best suicide is a sign of great weakness and a poor testimony to trusting in God's care.

8. "Can I sin without knowing it? Am I still accountable for sins I commit unawares?"

The answer is, "Yes." Sin labels any thought, word or deed that is not exactly in accordance with God's law. Our ignorance or misunderstanding of God's law does not alter the results of a comparison between our performance and the perfect standard of God's law. Acts 17:30 and I Timothy 1:13 do not excuse men. The verses simply remind us that God is patient with sinners who must repent. Disobedience is disobedience, a fact that is not canceled by our lack of conscious knowledge of the law's demands (Lev. 22:14-16, Josh. 20:1-5, Psalm 19:12).

As it turns out, we all have a conscience that tells us what is wrong and right (Rom. 2:14,15), even though it may be a scarred and twisted conscience. So our claim of ignorance is not completely valid.

We can be confused, forgetful or misled and thus go contrary to God's law. Yet it is still disobedience. And, if we are unsaved, we must give an account for the difference between our actions and the demands of God's law.

If we are saved, the good news is that God's sacrifice of Jesus covers all of our sins, those we know about and the ones we do not. We must keep in mind that salvation is a work of God alone and is not dependent upon our knowledge or effort. We are not asked to keep an accurate ledger of our sins in order to make sure we have asked for forgiveness for them all and are fully pardoned thereby. That attempt for completeness is a display of a gospel of works, that is, a salvation that is dependent upon something we do. Salvation is not equal to knowing all of our sins, repenting of all our sins and asking for forgiveness for all our sins. In fact, true believers will go to the grave not fully realizing the full extent of their disobedience. God alone realizes the extent of their disobedience, and pardons them fully for the sake of His Son, Jesus. That is a display of God's redeeming love and grace toward His children.

If we are saved but not mature in our understanding of God's Word, we can, in some matters, think incorrectly about what the Bible says. Our consciences may have been wrongly trained in the past and may continue that way until we mature in the Bible. However, if our hearts are right, we should follow our weak and distorted consciences, even if they give us wrong guidance. If we believe something to be right, whether it actually is or not, then we should not deliberately transgress what we think to be right because such an action would be rebellion (Rom 14:23). The reason is that why we do something is more important than what we do. Why we do something is a reflection of our heart attitude, but what we actually do is tempered by what we know.

Nevertheless, if we are truly saved, God will cause us to grow. Over time, God will reshape our consciences by means of His Word, a change that is welcomed by all true believers. Over time, God will renew our minds to conform to His, as we mature in our understanding of God's Word (Rom. 12:1-2).

Because Jesus has taken the penalty for all of our sins, we will not be judged for any actions that are not in accord with God's laws, whether we fully realize what we have done or not. The important thing is that we have hearts that seek to honor God and serve men. A right heart is a sign of salvation (Rom. 6:18).

9. "Will God allow a true believer to go far into sin?"

God deals with believers as a father does with children. Imagine that a father is in the front of his house working in the garden and his little child is playing near the sidewalk. The father may allow the child to wander a little way toward the street and the child may be scared by a large dog or a car that rushes by unexpectedly. But the father would not allow the child to be bit or enter the street and be hurt. Similarly, if we are God's child, and yet have a stubborn insistence in one area of our life, God may allow us that indulgence to a degree, even to our physical and mental harm, but never to our spiritual destruction. That principle is illustrated in the lives of Abraham, Lot, David, Peter and John Mark, among others.

God has His own reasons for dealing with each of His children in various ways. But as has been said, "experience keeps a dear school" and often we will learn in none other. Many lessons are thoroughly learned only in the school of "hard knocks." The lessons that God's people gain from the consequences of their own folly are often etched into their memories and stand them in good stead for future challenges, as well as help them convincingly explain God's ways to others.

However, if people who previously identified themselves with Christianity go completely away from the faith, it could be that they were never really saved in the first place, despite their apparent zeal and faithfulness. Their previous identification could have been based upon the fact they grew up in the church or maybe they thought they might gain some advantage associating with church members. If, on the other hand, people are truly saved, then their waywardness is part of their hard education in the harm and waste of sin. Eventually, God will draw those people back, sadder but wiser.

David's sinful, foolish dalliance with Bathsheba and his successful scheme to kill her husband would make anyone think that he was not saved, for who would imagine that God would allow one of his children to wander so far? Clearly, we cannot make an assessment about another person's spiritual condition based upon his outward behavior. God alone knows a man's heart. But a person who truly is saved will not make excuses or rationalizations when faced with his sin. After Nathan pointed out David's sin, the dagger of God's Word cut deeply and David bitterly repented of his sin. Even though the physical consequences remained, David's true love for God was revealed in the light of God's Word.

10. "Does God view the sin a Christian commits differently than the same sin committed by a non-Christian?"

In one sense the answer to the question is, "Yes." The sins that a Christian commits are covered by Jesus' atoning sacrifice. Jesus has paid for them all, past, present and future. God remembers them no more. So, there are no eternal consequences for the sins of a Christian. In contrast to that, the same sins committed by someone who is unsaved will be reviewed by God on Judgment Day, the result of which will be to consign him to eternal Hell.

In another sense the answer to the question is, "No." For one thing, the rules of God are the same for all. Christians and non-Christians must obey God. Christians must obey in gratitude and love for their Savior. Non-Christians must obey because they are God's creatures and accountable as people created in His image. The law of God does not disappear from the life of a person who has been saved by God's grace. A Christian cannot say, "free from the law, happy condition," if he means that he does not have to live by God's rules (Rom. 6:1-2). He is free from condemnation (Rom. 8:1), free from the obligation to obey the law in order to be right with God (Gal. 5:1) and free from the dominion of his sinful flesh (Rom. 6:17-18). However, any sin a believer commits is just as wicked as the same sin anyone else commits. In fact, his sin can be viewed as particularly horrid inasmuch as he sins despite having the resources at his disposal to resist its attraction, whereas as an unbeliever is spiritually dead and cannot respond to the commandments of God.

Also, the physical and mental consequences of sin are the same for both Christians and non-Christians. That means on this side of eternity, the physical and mental effects of sin are often indelible. To the general curse under which all people live, Christian and non-Christian alike, we can add the consequences of their foolish behavior. For example, an episode of sexual indiscretion can lead to a debilitating disease from which a person may suffer the rest of his life, whether he is saved or not saved. In another example, a man who is divorced and remarried damages the credibility of his counsel to other married people, even after he becomes saved.

The sins of a Christian and a non-Christian are equally expensive on this side of eternity. Sin often results in a loss of time, opportunity and human relationships. A Christian can repair some of the damage his sins cause, but there will always be a reminder of his past foolishness. This arrangement is God's will and a token of His care. The painful reminders of past sins that come to a Christian's mind serve to humble him. They also maintain and increase his appreciation for God's past and present grace, as well as draw him closer to his Lord.

11. "Should I ask for forgiveness from someone against whom I have sinned? Or do I just ask for God's forgiveness? What if the person is not aware that I have sinned against him?"

If the person is aware of your sin against him, then it might be right to ask for his forgiveness, depending upon the situation. For example, in a family, where people spend much time close together and know each other well, it is almost always appropriate to ask for forgiveness for sins committed between them. A husband should ask for forgiveness of his wife, and a wife of her husband. Parents should ask forgiveness of their children, and children of their parents.

Similarly, there are times to ask for forgiveness of co-workers and friends. But even in these cases, it is far better to repent before God, ask for His forgiveness, and take steps to change your thoughts, words and deeds, rather than rush to ask for forgiveness. A change in what you say and do sets the stage for peace between you and another person against whom you may have sinned. The reason a request for forgiveness may not be required is that a change in your words and actions will often resolve the problem and no further conversation is needed. Besides, a change in your words and actions is a lot more impressive Gospel witness and is usually necessary to ensure that your eventual contrite request for forgiveness will be taken seriously. Talk is cheap. People will be more likely to notice a clear and sustained change in you, even if you have not acknowledged and confessed the sinful words you may have said and the sinful actions you may have done.

If the other person does not know you have sinned against him in thought, word or deed, then it is best to talk to God alone about it and leave it with Him. Telling the other person could easily lead to his misunderstanding and may cause that person to have thoughts about you or the sin you committed that he should not think. For example, you should never encourage the attitude of self-justification in yourself or in another person, which an admission of guilt may cause. If you have repented and taken steps to change, then the problem is solved. Remember, ultimately your sin is against God, and you are accountable to Him alone, not to any man.

12. "Can I confess my sins to another person so that he can go to God and ask Him for forgiveness on my behalf? Can someone else pardon my sin as the representative of God?"

The answer to both questions is, "Absolutely no!" It is true that in James 5 we read the command "pray for one another." We can and should pray for other people. Abraham prayed for the city of Sodom (Genesis 18:23-32). A certain ruler prayed for his daughter (Matt. 9:18,19). But we must never pray in place of each other, as a proxy. Only God in the persons of Jesus and the Holy Spirit does that (Rom. 8:26,27, I Tim. 2:5, I John 2:2). Each person must come to God on his own to plead for God's mercy (Isaiah 55:6,7, Luke 18:13-14).

13. "When bad things happen to me, is God punishing me for my sins? When good things are denied or taken away from me, is it because I don't deserve them?"

The answer to the first question is, "No." But the reason why is different for non-Christians than for Christians. The bad things that happen to non-Christians are not punishments from God because the time for God's punishment of unsaved people has not yet come. Punishment of all unsaved people will be administered at the end of the world (Matt. 24:29-30, John 12:48, Rev. 6:13-17). We must keep in mind that punishment is the payment a person receives for the sins he commits (Matt. 12:36-37, Rev. 20:12-13). But that payment cannot be given until after his deeds have been examined in order to determine what he has earned. In other words, a trial must precede punishment. That trial, when God will examine the lives of all unbelievers, occurs on Judgment Day. Inasmuch as that great trial has not yet taken place, it is not possible for God to administer any punishment now.

In light of that, we can understand the bad things that non-Christians experience to be a result of God's general curse to which He subjected His universe and its inhabitants in answer to Adam's sin. Also, we can recognize the bad things that afflict people as consequences of their own particular foolish behavior. Furthermore, the bad things that happen to people who continue as unbelievers until the end of time serve to prepare them for the judgment to come. Unbelievers are prepared as they react in bitterness and despair to their problems, a reaction that reveals their wicked hearts and their unbelief.

In contrast to that, the bad things that happen to Christians are not punishments from God because God's time to punish those whom He saves has already come. In fact, true believers will never personally be punished for any of their sins because Jesus has taken all of their punishment upon Himself, which includes punishment for all of their past, present and future sins (I Peter 2:24).

It is true that people in authority on earth, such as parents or governmental officials, may punish who are under their jurisdiction. And they should, when it is appropriate. God has obligated them to punish (Prov. 22:15, Rom. 13:1-4). Among other things, any earthly punishment they dispense is a lesson that a man reaps what he sows. God wants His people to see a picture of His ultimate punishment at the end of time, in order that they might fear. God can use those earthly punishments to prepare the heart of an unbeliever for salvation. Also, God can use earthly punishments to make Christians walk more humbly. However, the earthly punishments Christians sometimes endure on earth now are not really punishments from God, that is, not in the sense that they are payment for the sins they commit.

In addition to that, some of the bad things Christians experience are totally unrelated to the idea of punishment, earthly or otherwise. For one thing, Christians can expect unbelievers of the world to abuse them because of their faithful life and testimony. For another thing,

Christians can expect "chastisement" from their Heavenly Father. That is, God's love is shown to His children in that He does not abandon them to their folly, but rather teaches them to walk away from sin and live more faithfully to Him (Heb. 12:6). Rather than giving them up to their own wicked devices, as He does unbelievers (Psalm 78:29, Rom. 1:24), God spanks his children through the hard experiences He sends their way in response to their sins. God teaches them valuable lessons thereby. The objective of the chastisement is not punishment, but the peaceable fruit of righteousness (Heb. 12:11). In that light, although we could say that chastisement is bad in the sense it is painful, it is not really a bad thing because it causes Christians to grow spiritually. In other words, Christians must understand that God works all bad things "for good to them that love God" (Rom. 8:28).

The second question can be answered in the following way. It is true, in general, that a person's behavior which conforms to the will of God tends to result in benefits for him. It is also true that a person's foolishness often causes him to miss a blessing. Furthermore, it is true that all men, Christians included, sin all of their lives on earth and do not deserve anything good. However, we must not think that God withholds or removes good things from a person because some of his particular sins make him unworthy of enjoying those good things. We must not make that kind of connection between a person's specific sins and the blessings of God. For example, a child must not think, "My mother died of cancer because I do not deserve a mother's care." Nor should a child think, "My mother and father divorced because I don't deserve to have any parents or a happy home." God does not deprive a child of his mother or father based upon what He sees in that child's heart and life. It is true that a child could do something accidentally or even deliberately that would naturally lead to his mother's death. Or a child could be such a problem that it adds to the strain between his parents. But God does not remove a child's parent in death or allow a child's parents to divorce as a way to show the child he is not worthy of a normal family.

For one thing, many of the bad things that happen to a person and many of the good things that are denied a person cannot be automatically related to his particular sins. After all, there are factors which shape a person's life on earth that are known only to God. The best way to analyze the experiences in a person's life is through the lens of the Gospel. If a person is not a believer, then God may give good things to him or remove good things from him in order to prepare him for judgment or call him to His Kingdom (Rom. 2:4-5). If a person is a true believer, then God works all things together for his spiritual benefit, now and into eternity (Gen. 50:20, Prov. 12:21).

For another thing, the good things that come to a Christian are not related his own work but to the grace of God. Again, no one really deserves any benefits of family or health that come from God, benefits that many people take for granted. Any blessing a Christian happens to receive in his life is a gift. God gives good things far beyond what anyone has a right to expect. He gives as a Father to His children, according to the love of His heart, expressed in the promises found in His Word, the greatest which is an eternity of fellowship with Him in Heaven.

14. "Are the wicked things I do just a result of being human?"

Yes, in one sense, it is true that "to sin is human." But no one can use that fact to excuse his sin. It does no good to complain, "I really can't help it, that's the way I am. Nobody is perfect. You just have to expect some sin in a human's life. I am doing the best that I can and it is unreasonable and unfair to demand anything more from me." Of course sinners can't help it. Of course that is the way they are. However, that is the problem for which the Gospel was designed and brought to earth in Jesus. What a sinner cannot do, God can. God calls people to seek Him while He may be found. In that way they may find the supernatural motivation and power to turn from sin and obey God.

Is important to recognize that people are not sinners because they are human. Being human is not the crime for which people are condemned. After all, Adam and Eve were human and without sin before the Fall. Not only that, Jesus was fully human, but He never sinned (Heb. 2:14, 4:15, I John 3:5). The problem is not that all people are part of the human race but that they are part of a **fallen** human race. The sin of people is not a testimony to their design but to the fact that something is wrong with their hearts and souls.

It is not as if Adam and Eve were created sinful. Originally God created Adam as a perfect creature. Only after that, Adam sinned. Consequently, Adam died in his soul and became a sinner, that is, a person dominated by the sinful desires in his flesh. Then, Adam passed that sinful nature on to his descendants (Rom. 5:12). Thus, the fundamental problem is not that people are human but that they are corrupted and enslaved by sin. So today to be human means to be a sinner. This does not excuse us or provide a defense. It is just a fact.

I also would like to add that we do not share the guilt of Adam's particular sin of eating the forbidden fruit. Nevertheless, we are Adam's offspring, and each person inherits his cursed human nature because, according to the principle of creation, kind begets kind. All humans now are like their sin-corrupted father Adam. Also, like Adam, all people are created accountable to God so that the blame for any imperfection must be laid upon them and not upon God. Therefore, all people are trapped in the human race but are not off the hook. In addition to the condemnation that must come upon them because of who they are as part of the human race, they are condemned for all of their own personal sins that their fallen human nature causes them to deliberately commit.

Incidentally, we cannot use Matthew 26:41, which says, "Watch and pray, that ye enter not into temptation: the spirit indeed is willing, but the flesh is weak," as an excuse. Human weakness is not a reason for a person to justify himself. Certainly, people are not physically, morally and mentally strong enough to do all that they want to do or all they ought to do. They are weaker than they were originally designed to be because of God's general curse upon the universe. Also they are weakened as a result of their own sinful behavior. However, unsaved people are not just frail; they are spiritually dead. Sin is disobedience against God that has resulted in and is the evidence of a spiritually dead soul.

15. "Are people wicked because they have been improperly taught? Are the evil things people do the result of the fact that they have been raised without the benefit of Christian instruction and so do not know the right thing to do?"

The answer to these questions is, "No." Sin is not a result of ignorance. People know in their hearts what God requires of them (Rom. 2:14-15). They simply do not want to do it. Neither can people's unrighteousness be corrected by education. In fact, education is often used to support their evil rebellion. People use what they learn about the universe in order to be more imaginative in their sin and more successful in fulfilling their own selfish desires. Education gives people the ability to sin more cleverly and effectively.

Certainly, sinful behavior can sometimes be arrested by making people aware of the dangerous consequences of their actions or by explaining to them the blessings that may result from their obedience. However, many times people will do what they want to do despite the harm or loss they know it brings to themselves and others. In the final analysis people do not operate upon the basis of facts and logic, but on the basis of their own foolish desires.

16. "Do people begin their lives as innocent children but lose their goodness by contact with a corrupt world? Are people at birth like clean slates, subsequently written upon by their evil environment?"

A person's wicked behavior may be controlled temporarily, in a limited way, through the influence of good examples. But a good example will not solve his sin problem. In fact, a good example only serves to highlight his own deficient record of behavior in the past and his unwillingness to obey in the present. There is no human way to acquire goodness from the environment. Real and permanent goodness comes only through the transforming power of God's grace as a result of salvation in Jesus Christ. So, the only way we can say that sin is the absence of good is to recognize that God alone is good and a life without Him is a life of sin.

The environment certainly contributes to the corruption of men both in the sense that one person encourages wicked behavior in another person and in the sense that the cursed universe is a source of frustration, anger and fear to each person who lives in it. But the origin of men's troubles is not "out there" someplace. It is within themselves, in their own wicked hearts. As we mentioned before, people are not victims of a foreign, sinful invasion. They are willing and eager participants in rebellion against God.

Although people's sin problems come from within, their help comes from without. They must seek the Savior who has come into the world to rescue sinners from God's wrath and the misery of sin. In a manner of speaking, Jesus is the only Person in the environment who can remove their sin.

17. "What about our physical diseases, as well as our emotional and psychological sicknesses? Shouldn't we be concerned about and deal with them, too? Aren't they just as much a problem for us as our sins?"

It is true we are plagued by physical, emotional or psychological problems, and for some of us those problems are very serious. Those problems cause us much grief and hardship. Therefore, it is not surprising that we are concerned about our physical problems. In fact, the Bible recognizes that we have a concern for our bodies (Eph. 5:29).

III John 2 describes John's prayer for the physical health of a lady as part of his Christian concern for her. And Philippians 2:25-30 describe Paul's concern for the health of Epaphroditus, even though a full understanding includes the spiritual lessons of those verses.

However, the Bible teaches that sin is the cause of the physical corruption and desolation of this broken world (Gen. 3:19, Hosea 4:1-3). Sin also is the cause of the moral and psychological burdens its inhabitants must bear. All of our shameful, painful and sad experiences are results of sin, our own sins as well as the sins of others. We experience physical, mental and emotional misery as a result of sin, both in the sense that God has cursed the universe in which we live, and in the sense that we often reap the bitter fruits of our own evilly motivated disobedience of God's law. Therefore, the physical diseases as well as the emotional and psychological sicknesses we experience are not our real problems. Instead, they are consequences and symptoms of sin. Sin is the root source of our troubles and must be the focus of our greatest concern.

Let us assume, for the sake of discussion, that our physical problems were our main concern. Even then our highest priority would be to deal with our sins. One reason is that only when we turn away from our sins can we hope to arrest and partially repair the physical and social damage that they have caused. That is how the physical universe is designed. For example, when a person turns away from drinking alcohol, he often can experience better physical heath and a happier family life. And yet, the physical improvement is not always certain or predictable. Even though God does send physical blessings to all His creatures, He does not guarantee them. God does not promise physical benefits to people who turn away from a particular sin. It may be that it is God's will for people to continue to taste the bitter fruit of their sins in order to accomplish His purposes. Nevertheless, on a physical level, it is generally true that a man reaps what he sows.

A second reason is that only when we turn from sin by means of the Gospel will our bodies have a hope of relief from the curse to which God has subjected His universe. That is, when we are saved and reveal it through a God-given desire and power to repent of our sins, we have the promise that our bodies will be raised incorruptible (I Cor. 15:52-53). This is a spiritual promise and not a physical promise because "flesh and blood cannot inherit the kingdom of God" (I Cor. 15:50). Nevertheless, we have the promise that our bodies will have a share in the future restoration of God's creation (Rom. 8:19-23).

A third reason is that, if we have not dealt with our sins in the

Gospel, any physical health we might receive in response to treatment for our physical, emotional and psychological problems is temporary and vain. In time we will all die of some physical problem, unless Jesus returns before. In fact, if we have not dealt with our sins in the Gospel, that is, if we are not saved, we will use any physical vitality and abilities we have to sin even more.

In conclusion, even if we had a physical concern and wanted solutions to our physical problems, we must keep in mind that sin is the power behind the physical terror and destruction that wreaks people's lives. No matter what our concern, we must deal with our sins.

And yet, the correct answer to the questions above is, "No." The proper cry of a person who is suffering from a physical disease, an emotional problem or psychological sickness, first of all should be, "I said, LORD, be merciful unto me: **heal my soul**; for I have sinned against thee (Psalm 41:4)." Our greatest concern always must be to find relief for our spiritual problems. Our concern for our sins must be far greater than our concern for any physical problem we may have.

The Bible declares that we are born dead in our trespasses and sins (Eph. 2:1). That is, if we are unsaved, we are dead in our souls and are under cruel bondage to the demands of our sinful flesh. The Bible also decrees that if we are not protected by Jesus' redemption, we will personally experience judgment, condemnation and eternal wrath (John 3:36, 5:28,29). Those spiritual perils are far more serious than the physical, emotional or psychological problems we may endure in this world as a consequence of our sins.

18. "How are we to understand the phrases 'backsliding Christian' and 'carnal Christian' that are used by some people today?"

The Bible uses the words, "backslider," "carnal" and "Christian." But the Bible never combines the words "backslider" or "carnal" with the word "Christian. If a person is truly a Christian, then he cannot also be called "a backslider" or "carnal."

It is true that a Christian continues to sin, sometimes grievously, as in the case of king David. But stating that such a Christian is a "backslider" or "carnal" is saying more than the Bible allows. Let us see how the Bible uses these words and why they cannot be applied to a Christian.

God called Israel a "backsliding" nation because it "played the harlot" (Jer. 3:6) and committed spiritual "adultery" (Jer. 3:8). God said the same of Judah (Jer. 3:8,14). God's solution was salvation (Jer.

4:4,14). That is, the two backsliding nations needed salvation. Although God spoke of nations, He referred to the rebellious individuals in the nations, and not to the faithful people in those nations (as Jeremiah). From this we see that God uses the word "backsliding" to refer to someone who acts unsaved because they are unsaved and so needs to be saved. "Backsliding" is not a word that applies to someone who is saved.

The word translated "carnal" refers to the physical part of a person. It is not a sin in itself to have a physical part, for Jesus did and yet had no sin (Heb. 4:15). However, ever since Adam, a person's carnal part is the residence of his sinful desires (Rom. 7:18). Saved and unsaved people have a carnal part. If that was all they had we could call all people carnal. However, the complete story is that every person also has a non-carnal or spiritual part, which we can call his soul. An unsaved person's soul is dead in sin (Eph. 2:1), so his carnal part dominates his thinking and behavior, unrestrained by his dead spiritual part. On the other hand, a saved person's soul is alive with the life of Jesus (Gal. 2:20). That spiritual life is stronger than the desires of his carnal part. While a Christian's carnal and spiritual parts struggle against each other (Gal. 5:17), his spiritual part eventually triumphs and causes him to think and act as God wills (Gal. 5:16,24,25).

Now we see why the Bible never uses the phrase "carnal Christian" because that would imply something that is not true, namely, that the word "carnal" describes him, that he is dominated by his carnal part. It is true that a Christian can disobey God in a particular instance or for a short space of time walk similarly to an unsaved person. But a true Christian does not continue unhindered in the specific sin against which he is struggling. In time God will arrest him in his sinful pursuits and turn him so that he walks as he should. Over time, it is clear that there is a difference between a Christian's and a non-Christian's walk. Therefore, the Bible never uses the word "carnal" to refer to a Christian.

God called some in the Corinthian congregation "carnal" because they "walk as men," that is, as men guided by their sinful desires alone (I Cor. 3:3). No further modifying comment was made about their souls because they acted like they were carnal and only carnal, without any spiritual life. Actually the word "carnal" was a general statement directed toward the whole congregation and the Holy Spirit applied it to the individuals as He saw fit. True believers examined themselves and saw the evidence of God's grace in their lives. Unbelievers were either hardened or broken before God's word of admonition.

We should mention that Paul referred to himself as "carnal' (Rom. 7:14). However, while he recognized that he was human with a carnal part (Rom. 7:18) he continued, explaining that he had a part that delights in God's law (Rom. 7:22). That is, we could say that Paul was a walking civil war (Rom. 7:23). However, his spiritual part eventually triumphed over his flesh in the particular sin against which he was fighting (Rom. 7:25). When God uses the word "carnal" alone, without any further comment, He identifies someone who walks like an unsaved person because they are unsaved. But that was not Paul's situation.

Some people use the terms "backsliding Christian" or "carnal Christian" to help them explain why a person who makes a public profession of faith in Jesus and, for a while, outwardly acts in an apparently spiritual way, later on falls away from the faith. The terms are based upon their view that a person is saved when he makes a public confession of sin and announces his faith in Jesus as his personal Savior, and that he can be considered to be saved based upon that confession, no matter what his subsequent pattern of behavior may be.

That view of salvation is misleading. Since we cannot see into a person's soul, we do not know the spiritual situation of anyone based upon anything he does. He may be truly saved or just a phony. If a person is walking in obvious sin, it may be that he is saved and God allowed to stray in order to teach him some hard lessons. We have already mentioned the example of king David, to which we could add the story of the apostle Peter. But if a person is saved, it eventually will become evident, as God calls him back to the faith and restores him to fellowship. A saved person will demonstrate spiritual growth in various areas of his life over time because he has Jesus' resurrected life within him. That growth will continue until his last day on earth. So a saved person cannot be called a "backsliding Christian" or a "carnal Christian." On the other hand, if a person continues to live as an unbeliever without any change from his former unsaved life or without any significant difference from the life of those people who claim to be unbelievers, then in all likelihood he is unsaved and his prodigal life reflects the true nature of his heart (Matt. 7:18-20). In that case he is a "backslider" because he has returned to his sin dominated life, as we read in II Peter 2:22. He is "carnal" because he has no spiritual life.

Afterword

In the Bible we read, "There is none righteous, no not one ..... for **all have sinned**" (Rom. 3:10,23). And to all sinners the Bible threatens an unimaginably horrible punishment, that is inevitable, certain, and without appeal or end (Psalm 76:7, Nahum 1:6-9, Matt. 25:46, Luke 16:26, II Thess. 1:9).

So, whether we recognize it or not, whether we want to recognize it or not, the Bible declares that we are sinners. But that is **good news**. Because Jesus said, "I am not come to call the righteous, but **sinners** to repentance" (Matt. 9:13). Even though sinners are in danger of punishment, it does not have to be that way. There is hope for sinners, as we read in I Timothy 1:15, "This is a faithful saying, and worthy of all acceptation, that Christ Jesus came into the world to **save sinners**."

The Bible is a good friend because it tells us the truth about ourselves. And the Bible is a good comforter because it tells us of God's promised Savior. The Bible's call goes out to the sinners of the world,

"He that covereth his sins shall not prosper: but whoso confesseth and forsaketh them shall have mercy." Prov. 28:13

"Seek ye the LORD while he may be found, call ye upon him while he is near: Let the wicked forsake his way, and the unrighteous man his thoughts: and let him return unto the LORD, and he will have mercy upon him; and to our God, for he will abundantly pardon."

Isaiah 55:6,7

For all who have been forgiven, the Bible declares:

"Bless the LORD, O my soul: and all that is within me, bless his holy name. Bless the LORD, O my soul, and forget not all his benefits: Who forgiveth all thine iniquities; who healeth all thy diseases; Who redeemeth thy life from destruction; who crowneth thee with lovingkindness and tender mercies; Who satisfieth thy mouth with good things; so that thy youth is renewed like the eagle's. The LORD executeth righteousness and judgment for all that are oppressed. He made known his ways unto Moses, his acts unto the children of Israel. The LORD is merciful and gracious, slow to anger, and plenteous in mercy. He will not always chide: neither will he keep his anger for ever. He hath not dealt with us after our sins; nor rewarded us according to our iniquities. For as the heaven is high above the earth,

so great is his mercy toward them that fear him. As far as the east is from the west, so far hath he removed our transgressions from us. Like as a father pitieth his children, so the LORD pitieth them that fear him. For he knoweth our frame; he remembereth that we are dust. As for man, his days are as grass: as a flower of the field, so he flourisheth. For the wind passeth over it, and it is gone; and the place thereof shall know it no more. But the mercy of the LORD is from everlasting to everlasting upon them that fear him, and his righteousness unto children's children; To such as keep his covenant, and to those that remember his commandments to do them. The LORD hath prepared his throne in the heavens; and his kingdom ruleth over all. Bless the LORD, ye his angels, that excel in strength, that do his commandments, hearkening unto the voice of his word. Bless ye the LORD, all ye his hosts; ye ministers of his, that do his pleasure. Bless the LORD, all his works in all places of his dominion: bless the LORD, O my soul."

Psalm 103:1-22